W9-CNS-241

A NAZI
CHILDHOOD

A NAZI
CHILDHOOD

᠍᠍

Winfried Weiss

mosaic press

Canadian Cataloguing in Publication Data

Weiss, Winfried, 1937-91
A Nazi childhood

ISBN 0-88962-727-4

1. Weiss, Winfried, 1937-91 - Childhood and youth. 2. World War,
1939-45 – Personal narratvies, German. 3. World War, 1939-45 –
Children – Germany. 4. Children – Germany – Biography. I. Title.

D811.5.W44 2001   940.53'161   C2001-930300-9

No part of this book may be reproduced or transmitted in any form, by any
means, electronic or mechanical, including photocopying and recording, information storage and retrieval systems, without permission in
writing from the publisher, except by a reviewer who may quote brief
passages in a review.

Published by Mosaic Press, offices and warehouse at 1252 Speers Road,
Units 1 and 2, Oakville, Ontario, L6L 5N9, Canada and Mosaic Press, PMB
145, 4500 Witmer Industrial Estates, Niagara Falls, NY, 14305-1386,
U.S.A.

Mosaic Press acknowledges the assistance of the Canada Council and the
Department of Canadian Heritage, Government of Canada for their support
of our publishing programme.

Copyright © 2001 The Estate of Winfried Weiss
ISBN 0-88962-727-4

Printed and Bound in Canada.

MOSAIC PRESS, in Canada:
1252 Speers Road, Units 1 & 2,
Oakville, Ontario
L6L 5N9
Phone/Fax: 905-825-2130
mosaicpress@on.aibn.com

MOSAIC PRESS, in U.S.A.:
4500 Witmer Industrial Estates
PMB 145, Niagara Falls, NY
14305-1386
Phone/Fax: 1-800-387-8992
mosaicpress@on.aibn.com

Le Conseil des Arts | The Canada Council
du Canada | for the Arts

ᛝ PREFACE ᛝ

Life began in the sticky genes of history long before I was born. There was evidence to prove it. It was in my father's desk, in the upper right-hand drawer where he kept our family photo album, my mother's memory book, and a chart of our ancestors.

I can't think of a time when I didn't know the contents of my father's drawer. Even when I couldn't read I knew what was inside. I had memorized the pages in these books, and associated the past with the hieroglyphics, which my parents had written. And, on rainy days or when I was sick, I read in the atmosphere of these three documents the way others read God in the Bible. I solemnly turned the pages and looked at their mystic contents until I was gorged with the pictures, names, and history of the past that had led up to me.

Our photo album had a checkered cover. The pages were black and my father had neatly dated each picture in white ink, gothic script. Between the pages was thin tissue paper, which rustled like candy wrapping. History for me was wrapped in crisp, crinkling sounds. It surrounded my grandfather on a bicycle in front of a fake landscape, 1978, and it sounded like radio static in the swastikas that fluttered above the swimming pool in Munnerstadt, with my mother standing in its shallow end, 1935. It crackled in the forest where my father was kneeling next to a buck he had shot, 1930, and it made background noises for my sisters and my mother taking a Sunday walk through the Franconian fields, 1936. And the tissue paper made the only sounds for a quiet portrait of my father in his black SA-uniform, looking stern and official, early in 1937, just months before I arrived on the scene I penetrated the photo album to find myself. The past didn't have color; it lived in sepia-tinted forests, black and white villages, and glossy gardens. It was full of dark and light contrasts, with cozy shadows. I was hidden in them. My father had neatly ordered the past so that it led up to me in 1937 when I made my appearance in the album. The images before me were a preparation for my entrance. I, so it appeared to me, was the exclamation point at the end of a long sentence.

My mother's memories had a red cover. They had gilded pages and the gold came off on my fingers. The paper had brown age spots on it. The pages were musky; past time had a pungent smell; it escaped into the air every time I opened the book. In it were people's memories of memories that had preceded me. My mother's book had no photographs but it had pictures and verses of her friends that became mine, because I was her son. Someone had drawn a rose and written next to it: "The world is lonely and cold;

youth, like the rose, dies in the summer night..."
and, "Remember forever our picnics — Your
friend Dora, March 1920." March had a tiny
brown fly stuck to it. I could see the spidery legs
spread out in all directions, broken and distorted.
The small insect had made a dark stain on the
creamy paper. Through the squashed fly I stared
into 1920. Behind the insect-screen I saw my
mother talk with her friend Dora. They were
walking under a moon of summer flowers
between the book's pages. A yellow rose and a
small blue crocus. The crocus was paper-thin and
had strong veins. I held the flowers up to my
nose to smell the past, my prehistory. The past
smelled like old straw. I finally added my own
verse in my mother's book:

I wish you a lot of roses
and blooming meadows all your life,
until someone in trousers
asks you to be his wife.
                    Your loving son Winfried
                    February 12,1945

I was barely able to write then. I made the
entry two years after my father had disappeared,
and sometimes I saw him just like one of the
flower stalks in the memory book, a memory
squeezed by time.

I was Aryan to the bone. Long before my
father's pushy sperm conquered my mother's

floating egg to make me, he filled out a long official chart on creamy-white paper. It was the rough draft for the original, which was sent off to the center for racial purity in Munich.

When neatly folded according to instructions, the word AHNENTAFEL appeared in heavy gothic script on the top. Underneath was written: for proof of Aryan ancestry. The fat black print of AHNENTAFEL was like a heavy lid under which my father's impeccable gothic script had preserved two hundred years of pure Germanic history, in thirty slim boxes. The boxes were jars and my ancestors fermented in them like plum schnapps. Every time I looked at them shaped in my father's handwriting, I felt them pushing out of their chart and escaping into the room like balloons that had suddenly inflated. They floated around me, watching me, their culmination. I saw them as dark people through my father had told me that our name originated with one of our ancestors who was particularly blond and light-looking compared to Jews who had the same name. They got their names in the nineteenth century; they didn't have any names then, and they had to go to city hall where clerks gave them names. Often the clerks couldn't think of names and picked any color that came to their mind. I asked why my father had such dark hair and they told me that was because he came from close to the Bohemian border where people were dark, and we had some Bohemian blood in us. I asked my

Aunt Anna, who had a little squint, why we had this long chart and she told me we had it because the government wanted to know who was Aryan and who was Jewish. The Jews came from faraway places they weren't supposed to come from, but we came from England! We had fought in the Hundred Years War and then drifted off into Germany to become robber barons and millers with big mills.

Our chart only went back to 1765 where it began with a servant at the courts of Amberg, a man called Joseqhus Adler who had a son called George who made a child with a woman called Anna Maria Weiss and didn't marry her. My Aunt Anna skipped over this fact, but my father explained that we really ought to be called Adler, and it was too bad that we got the mother's name, because Adler was such a poetic name. It came from an ancestor who caught eagles for a living. Jews on the other hand who had the same name got it because they bribed officials to get a nice name, that's what Tante Anna said. And, she said, she preferred to rely on her own information about our ancestors, because parish records could make mistakes. She didn't think much of the charts. Once I heard her whisper to my mother over a cup of chamomile tea that our chart was a disgrace. Illegitimate children were like a disease in it. It was a real epidemic! Even Uncle Fritz, my father's brother, was illegitimate! My mother said "shhh!" but Tante Anna went on.

Uncle Fritz and his father were both born out of wedlock, as well as his mother, my grandmother. But she had to admit that Uncle Fritz turned out to be a respectable postal inspector in Straubing on the Danube: he had five legitimate children. Two of them were officers in the German Army, one was a leader in the Hitler Youth, and the two girls were active in the BDM, the *Bund Deutscher Madchen.*

Aunt Anna said that we came from healthy stock. All of my ancestors lived in the country, and they grew to be very old because they led simple lives. She pointed to my father and said that he was another healthy example. All he had for lunch when he was a child were two hot boiled potatoes that his parents gave him in the morning before he set off on a long walk to school. He kept one in each pocket, ate them with a little bit of salt, and warmed his hands on them in the wintertime.

My father had figured out the average lifespan of my ancestors and noted the number in pencil on the reverse side of the chart: 67.384615 years. He also told me that they all married late. None of the men in the past 200 years had married before the age of thirty. The men married around thirty-five, and the women at twenty-seven. And, my father said, the record was held by my mother's father who had married my grandmother when he was forty-five. He was born in 1839. In his sepia tinted photographs he had a big gray Kaiser Wilhelm beard.

The past! The thin old women that walked like shadows in the streets of villages; widows wore black clothes — long black skirts that they never changed. They were like our charts. Opening our chart was like lifting the widow's skirts. My ancestors flew out like birds! Millers, farmers, farmhands, tailors, masons, miller's daughters, laborers, and peasants. Under these skirts it smelled like boiled potatoes, horse manure, the insides of pigs just slaughtered, like hot crusty summer soil in which the potatoes were growing. And it smelled like *bratkartoffeln*, cold boiled potatoes that were fried in lard with caraway seeds on top. All the farmers ate them in the evening, and the smell was all over the house and had gotten into my picture of the past hidden in the widow's skirts. My ancestors were stewing in smells I knew from the villages, and I came out of them too.

All of this, then, served to inspire the tale that follows...

℞ PROLOGUE ℞

I was a spectacular Aryan baby. When I was born I weighed nine German pounds. I had blonde hair and blue eyes. I was perfect. They left me the way I had come into the world — nobody thought of snipping off my long and healthy foreskin because circumcision was a suspect alien ritual.

I had a father, a mother, and two sisters. We lived in the midst of the fields and meadows of Franconia, surrounded by fat cows and big dung heaps, right in the geographical center of the German Reich. I was like a baby rooster crowing in the cradle while the women of the house sat around me like clucking hens discussing the best recipes for making *Kartauserklosse*, big dumplings boiled in a napkin.

Seasons came and went; everybody was happy. My hair turned a shade brown, my eyes green. I grew big and strong, just like Germany. My mother kept house, my father did his job. They didn't bother too much with politics. They loved us, and my father rocked me on his knees in the evening before I went to bed. One day he would show me how to grow up! My sisters would marry, I would go out into the world, my parents would move into their little *Häuschen* for which they had started to save, and drive around in their Volkswagen as Hitler had promised.

And then one day my Father went to Russia and never came back. It was so long ago that I can't remember whether I loved him. But I do remember that I loved my mother so much that, had she died, I would have died with her.

Just before he went to Russia my father joined the SS and

1

had his blood group tattooed in his armpit. The first thing the Russian guerillas did was check for tattoos. My mother's friends whispered to each other but I could not hear them. "Russians killed Germans on the spot. They gouged out their eyes and cut off their testicles. Russians were beasts. Beasts!" they said with strong intonations, while they rattled their cups and saucers, stirring with their spoons. My father was an open wound in the Russian snows. My mother's mouth puckered and quivered. She cried and asked why nobody could tell her if my father was dead or alive. Missing in action was worse than death. I looked at her out of the corner of my eyes and I was embarrassed. I had heard the phrases so often that I knew them by heart. "Poor Germany," she said. And that it had come to this! Why did this happen to us? We hadn't done anything. And now she was a widow with three children on her hands. A widow was prey to the world. She was a hare hunted by hounds. And the ladies that still had their husbands nodded their heads and said, "Ja! Ja! It was simply *Schrecklich! Schrecklich!*" The sound of the word sealed my fate.

PART I

To my mother and Franconia

℞ 1 ℞

My mother had a solemn face. She said, "You stirred for the first time at the open grave of your grandmother!" I looked with her right into that open grave. I knew I had to wait for the grave to close before she would continue the story of my birth. I had a dark beginning.

My grandmother was buried on a cold and snowy day in February 1937. I, the swirling tiny mass of protoplasm, sperm, egg, and protein, just conceived, began to pulse inside my mother and make her sick. She had stomach cramps and had to leave the funeral before it was over.

All of this happened in Münnerstadt where my mother had been born, a small medieval town with towers and fortified walls. My mother went to her dead mother's house and rested on the small couch in the parlor next to the store where my grand mother sold groceries, flowers, venison, and anything else that was profitable, and had saved a modest little fortune. While my mother waited to get better, she breathed in the smell of dried goods, waxed floors, and musky vegetables stored in the huge dark hall outside. And I breathed in the smells too.

At this point of the tale my mother made an indifferent face; she wasn't sure how she felt about the little protein-ball inside her. I scrutinized her face. After all, she said, she was thirty-eight, my father, thirty-nine; they already had two daughters, Ilse and Gertrude, and she didn't want to start all over again with diapers and sleepless nights. But, she then said, my father was happy; he wanted a male child. My mother smiled at me, and I always was relieved because I had made it! The story could go on.

• • •

And so I grew from February to November. Spring came, then summer, warm but not too hot as it always was in Pfarrweisach, Northern Franconia, the very last part of Bavaria, not far from Bamberg to the south and Bayreuth to the east.

Wheat fields, forests, pastures, rolling hills, and wonderful baroque castles and medieval ruins were all around me.

When I was ripening like a Franconian apple, a pear, or even a turnip inside my mother, my father was a policeman. He belonged to the gendarmerie, a police unit in charge of the countryside. We lived in an apartment in an immense old house that once belonged to the Castle of Lichtenstein, but now was owned by the Kuhns, a family of farmers. Mr. Kuhn, who loved to ride horses, had just decided to join the SS because the SS had the only riding club in the area. His black riding boots made crisp echoing sounds on the old tiles in the hall as I was sucking away at my umbilical cord, taking as much as I could out of my mother. Hitler built more and more planes, and my father received the SA-Sport medal in bronze. It had the number 001249806. The number is right under the phrase, "In the name of the Führer." The photograph shows my father in a black uniform. He has very short hair and is wearing all kinds of decorations on his left side. It's a bad picture of him; his skin looks leathery and unreal because the photographer tried to touch it up.

The pictures of that year show my mother and sisters in summer dresses sitting in meadows, next to rivers, or in a clearing in the forest. They smile into my father's black Agfa. My sisters have pageboy haircuts; we have a spaniel (who once gave my sister Gertrude a worm); my mother is holding a wide white hat in her hands, or she is smelling some flower. Her dress is hiding me; I was listening at the walls of her placenta.

So our life went on in Franconia. Everybody lived happily in the valleys and forests of 1937. My father did his duty, my mother looked after the household. My father was promoted again; like previous promotions this one is announced on heavy, first quality, cream-colored paper, signed by the president of the German Gendarmerie, and under the "*Heil Hitler!*" is Hitler's printed signature.

My mother went to meetings of the National Socialist Women's movement where they exchanged cooking recipes and sang German songs while they knitted socks for the poor. She heard lectures on the sacred mission of the German woman. Since I was on the way she was especially prone to poetic ideas of German motherhood and its contribution to a new Europe. For many years, while I was growing up, she kept saying that mothers are sacred beings. I believed her. Through my mother's blood flowed songs about German linden trees, sacred oak groves where Wotan was worshiped, and through my mother's belly I heard lectures on Germanic burial sites in northern Franconia. The stage was set for me. I was going to slip out into a green, healthy, and poetic world.

• • •

On November 9, 1937, Pfarrweisach celebrated its *Kermesse*. The farmers came from the surrounding areas to drink in the two pubs and buy things at the booths in the

7

market square. My father was in the countryside keeping order, my sisters were in school, and my mother was puttering around the house when I decided to pull my umbilical cord. It was cold and foggy outside, but I was going to brave it. I had stayed longer than anticipated inside anyhow. My mother went into labor.

She did what any woman in labor pains did in Pfarrweisach: she went after Frau Schütz, the local midwife who lived at the other end of the village. Hebamm Schütz was famous. She cut the best navels in all of Northern Franconia. Beautifully recessed, healthy navels were her trademark. Years later, whenever my mother talked about Pfarrweisach, she always remembered Frau Schütz, always ending with "she was the best navel snipper in Northern Franconia!"

And it was true! All my life I admired the perfection of my navel, a cleanly snipped-off remnant of the umbilical cord, hidden and protected in its hollow like a rosebud that could blossom any moment and give off a wonderful fragrance.

On November 9, 1937, when my mother reached Frau Schütz, she was making soup from a sow they had slaughtered that day. My mother found her over a huge kettle in the midst of steam and the smell and swell of blood sausages. Next to half of the pig's carcass, which was hanging from a hook, my mother explained to her that I had decided to come out, and that her labor pains were already very strong.

Frau Schütz was not only a midwife; she also doubled as a butcher. After somebody had hit the pig over the head with a heavy club, she cut the neck arteries and caught the blood in big pans for blood sausages, then she slashed open the belly to take out the insides. Her hands were bloody and steaming, my mother told me. Sometimes the pig still squealed while she took out the heart and the liver. Frau Schütz was a real professional in both jobs.

On November 9 she wasn't happy to see my mother. She told her that she always slaughtered her own pigs on Kermesse Day and why did I have to pick that day for getting born? Then she gave my mother a quick examination next to the dead Franconian sow and rows of sausages from the last hog. I could have been born right there, but I was discreet and waited. Frau Schütz said that I wouldn't come until 2 a.m., the next morning. Frau Schütz was never wrong. She had a real knack for estimating births, and was as swift and correct in announcing them as she was in cutting umbilical cords and pigs and my mother went back home to take hot foot baths and drink strong coffee as the midwife had told her to do.

Everything took its course. My sisters went down to the Kuhns after being told that the stork was going to bring them another baby. My older sister sneered, but my younger one looked out of windows all evening long. My mother didn't interrupt her usual routine; she cooked dinner for my father and held on to the furniture when the labor pains came.

•   •   •

What was I thinking when I floated along my mother's birth canal into Franconia? I have to rely on witnesses who say that when my father came home that evening and heard that I was on the way, he consulted the almanac to see what famous people had been born on November 10. He came up with Martin Luther and Friedrich Schiller, Germany's second greatest poet. They were satisfied. There was also a French composer of whom they had never heard, Couperin. He was like the frosting on the cake. *"Gut, gut!"* my father said, and threatened to go off to a political rally. But my mother told him to stay because he had been to political rallies for the previous two births. She had other reasons for keeping my father at home, suspecting that my father had taken a liking to the new *NS-Krankenschwester*, the official National Socialist nurse in charge of health in Pfarrweisach and the surroundings. She was called Ute Rüdenhof and wore her party button right over her heart.

My father stayed, but threatened to leave at once if it would be another little cunt! But my mother assured him that this time it was a boy, because her labor pains were unlike the previous ones.

Frau Schütz arrived after midnight. She was red in the face, breathed heavily, and smelled of spices, hot blood sausages, and slaughtered pig. She told my father to massage my mother's back. My mother was lying in the large, white, lacquered bed under a copy of Raphael madonna. On the other wall was a huge picture of Jesus about to enter Jerusalem. Jesus was dressed in a long blue robe and made his way past palm fronds into a white city. He was sitting on a donkey. I was all coiled up inside my mother ready to make my way into Pfarrweisach, waiting for the right moment.

Shortly after 2 a.m. Frau Schütz knew the time had come. My mother screamed and my father wanted to leave; but Frau Schütz said, *"Nix da!"* ("nothing doing!") and told him to watch my mother carefully now, since a woman was never more beautiful than at the moment she was giving birth.

While my mother contracted in a giant effort, I uncoiled like a loosened spring and slipped out of the uterus, through the slimy and distorted cervical canal, and finally through the vagina into Franconia where Frau Schütz's hands, that had just butchered a big sow, were waiting for me. My father, still wearing his black boots and green uniform was staring at me; Frau Schütz cut the umbilical cord and said it was a boy! I started to cry, as I was expected to do, but soon afterwards fell asleep because I was exhausted by my birth, and my mother did the same.

The Reich had a new subject! Next door in the Kuhns stable the cows mooed and the horses kicked the sides of their partitions in their sleep, standing up. Frau Schütz went home saying that it had been a long day. First the big sow and now this nine-pound boy!

🙎 2 🙎

I had hardly recovered from the ordeal of being born when the local band arrived in the little park below our windows to serenade my mother and me. It was November 10, at nine in the morning; a wet mist hung over Franconia, big fat drops formed on the bare branches of the Kuhns fruit trees. I was lying in a cradle, next to my mother, both of us trying to cope with the finality of our mutual separation. My father and my sisters — who had stayed home from school in my honor — went to the window and waved to the trumpets and trombones playing *"Hoch soll er leben"* and a shortened version of the "Blue Danube Waltz." My father thanked them and told them to have a drink on him at the Wirthaus Mildenberger; my mother cried.

My father was ecstatic. My entry into the world incited him to start a kind of diary for which he took an old unused

SA calendar for the year 1933. It was bound in black leather with the letters "SA" stamped on it in gold. The leaves were gilded; a red silken bookmark hung inside. When the calendar was closed it had the appearance of a prayer book. And into this black cover, in the space allotted for the month of September, next to the red entry *Reichparteitag* in Nürnberg, my father wrote with black ink: "November 10, 1937. I have a son. Stammhalter — assures continuation of the line — A man must have a son; never had such *Gefühle* (sensations)." After the word *Gefühle* my father made a long dash (which is called a *Gedankenstrich* — a thought line) and then: "I saw myself come out of the womb."

On the opposite page of my father's entry is a full-page photograph of Ernst Röhm, the leader of the SA. He is sitting with his hands folded in his lap, his veins prominently displayed. Röhm is wearing the Iron Cross over his heart on his military tunic, and his hair is neatly parted in the middle. Over his lips he has a moustache like my father, and on the left side of his full round face over a short muscular neck, are two shadowy scars. In years to come, whenever my mother showed me the entry celebrating my birth, she would point to Röhm and say: "He looked just like Baker Grubert down the street from us, *wie aus dem Gesicht geschnitten* — like twins, it's amazing, they had the same dimple in their noses..." And while she leafed through the rest of the book she would sigh and say: "It's already so long ago and so confusing. I can't think about it or I'll go crazy!" I had carefully watched the place where the pages closed over the writing. I thought I could feel the leather, cold and aromatic, crush against my cheeks.

To the outside world, my father gave no hint of his hidden self; he masked it successfully by drawing analogies for my birth from Germany's growing military power. He went around saying that I had been launched from my mother like one of our new submarines from its building pad. He boasted to a SA colleague that I had shot out of my mother like a torpedo from its tube.

It made my mother angry and she told him to shut up. I had made a cautious entry into this world, she said; after all, she should know! I had stuck out my head and sampled the air and then gone back in before deciding to come out for good. My father exaggerated, just like a man, and, she said, she was not a launching tube for torpedoes!

I, of course, had no idea about the two different versions of my birth that circulated in Pfarrweisach, where the new-born son of the local gendarme was big news. My father, after all, was the local authority; when his gendarme-green presence passed in the streets everybody pulled their hats, though he had a small salary.

●   ●   ●

In the afternoon of November 10, there was a meeting of the regional SA association in Ebern where my father's presence was required. He said that he had to tear himself away from me because they wouldn't accept any excuses. The weekend edition of the local *Ebern Kurier* carried a summary of the meeting under the permanent heading "National Socialist Events in the Country of Ebern: Reunion of the SA-Comradeship at the Hotel Black Emperor."

The article said that among seasonal flower arrangements and autumnal wreaths of German Oak, the Gauleiter Klüngelmann had presented a patriotic speech praising the loyal ranks of the SA and their invaluable contribution to the

13

Movement, and then touched on the topic of gradual elimination of non-Aryan influences from our German culture. I, cuddled warm and snug in my blue cradle in Pfarrweisach, where the chimneys puffed lazy smoke into the cold November air, had no personal connection with the Gauleiter and his speech. But one of the other speakers lifted a glass of Franconian wine in the direction of my father and announced my recent birth. And there I was, mentioned in the papers; copies of the *Ebern Kurier* went into the archives, the world could read me forever; my presence linked with Gauleiter Klüngelmann's name, which stood over me like a patron saint! Everybody applauded, the Gauleiter rose again, incited to do so by my innocence, congratulated my father and said — in the exact words of the *Kurier* — "A son with the genes of a German man of law and order and of a loyal SA-man was a treasured contribution to our nation!" With me my father had fulfilled his racial duty and he (the Gauleiter) hoped that he (my father) would produce more sons because the Movement needed Aryan stock to carry our spirit and revolution into alien territories! There followed prolonged and emotional applause.

Adults in uniforms and long black boots rose to cheer me, my father, and the fatherland. After the major reunion was over, my father and a group of old friends went out for a *Kameradschaftsabend* to a local pub where my father contributed a whole barrel of beer in my honor. They got loaded on local dark brown beer and my father had to get up all night long to relieve himself.

Meanwhile, my mother, lying in a big white bed, received visitors who came with presents for me. Frau Kuhn, who was interested in astrology, explained on a piece of paper to my mother that I was a Scorpio! It was the eighth sign, she said, and drew a little diagram while my mother nodded: fixed, watery, and feminine, it said. Scorpios were secretive, occult, and powerful if they wanted to be. They were still waters that ran deep, one never knew what lurked under the surface. And Scorpios were strange, bizarre; Frau Kuhn squinted her eyes. They had unusual desires, she said. My mother kept her index finger over her mouth.

Then the two women went on to names. Frau Kuhn said that I needed the right name because a Scorpio without the fitting name was uneasy for the rest of his life. Anything but Adolf, she said! That was too overused and it didn't have a patron saint; I wouldn't have a saint's day to celebrate. She suggested Otto or Hans, good Franconian names, but my mother had risen above Frau Kuhn, she wanted something more refined for me, something with color and historical substance. Germanic myths were in vogue and she asked my father and sisters to look up our book club copy of the *Nibelungenlied* for ideas.

For the next several days, my family ran through all the male names in the German national epic. They pronounced them out loud to see how they sounded: Volker, Siegfried, Günther, Hagen (who was too sinister, they thought, he had run Siegfried through with his lance), Giselher, Siegmund, Ortwein, Gernaot, Dankwart, Fudiger. They couldn't reach a decision. My youngest sister, Gertrude, wanted Giselher. Gisel-her, she emphasized each syllable. It sounded blonde and aristocratic. My older sister and my mother liked Gunther without the umlaut: it made the name archaic, masculine. My father thought Volker wasn't too bad because it wasn't too common, and it wasn't too unusual either. But Frau Kuhn called all the Teutonic names "*so'n Schmarrn*," "all bullshit." None of the names had a patron saint, none of them appeared

15

in the saints' calendar, and a boy needed a decent saint! They tried a compromise, something half-Christian and half-pagan, and hit upon Winfried. It was Teutonic and was the name of St. Boniface, the apostle of Germany. It was perfection. I could celebrate my patron's day on June 9, and Winfried went well with the sound of Ferdinand which was going to be my middle name, because that was the name of my godfather, a game warden and friend of my father.

As soon as my name was settled Frau Kuhn came upstairs to convert my name into numbers and tried to arrive at my future; name is fate, she said. And as soon she had left to feed the cows, my father called Frau Kuhn's demonstration of the astrological signs, hogwash. But my mother put her right index finger to her lips, indicating that she was in thought. Frau Kuhn was close to nature, she said, and told my father to remember that our landlady always felt a pull in her right knee when the white asparagus under the ground was ready to come out! Maybe our landlady was aware of unseen airborne currents that already played me like a stringed instrument…?

The fact is: around the time of my birth a silvery flying machine appeared high in foreign skies far to the west of Franconia, with the letters XB-15 painted on it. Its wings too wide, its motors underpowered, the airplane — unlike me — was aborted. But the XB-15 was only one stage of an extended pregnancy under various code names: 229 B and YB-17 came at the time of my slippage into Franconia close to its final magic cipher B-17, a magnificent masculine machine that made the heavens vibrate with four powerful engines.

Though the B-17's incubation period started long before my parents accidentally fused egg and sperm, history labored to produce me and the B-17 simultaneously. We belonged to the same generation. The B-17 (in spite of belonging to the enemy) was mine; in it floated my metaphysical needs, in it my childhood, which was soon to begin, soared into the skies. The B-17 would be God, emitting condensation trails in the heavens over Franconia.

But in November 1937, I was still years away from the coming of the B-17; we were building our own *Luftwaffe*, and Hitler was making speeches in the same month about cramped Germans needing more open spaces, especially to the east.

•   •   •

I was baptized on November 15, a gloomy foggy day; I was dressed in warm blues, covered by a blanket Frau Kuhn had made from her own sheep wool. A small cold procession followed my parents and me to St. Kilian's where, five days after Frau Schütz had cleaned me from the filmy remnant of my mother's body, I was going to be cleansed of the sticky film of Original Sin.

St. Kilian, the patron saint of Pfarrweisach, had come with two companions — St. Kolonat and St. Totnan — to Franconia and Christianized it in the seventh century. Like most saints, they were killed by the natives, thus ensuring that their memory was kept alive. Every child in Pfarrweisach knew the saints' history because of a local custom: the teachers caned their charges to the rhythmical intonation of "that's for St. Kilian, that for St. Totnan, and take that for St. Kolonat."

St. Kilian's, the parish church, was built around 1500, and had an onion-shaped tower, the influence of the crusades. The gothic pillars were inscribed with the date 1511. In the north corner was buried Heinz von Rauhneck under

17

gray-green sandstone, with the inscription, "Here lies a good squire who died on the Saturday after Easter in the 4th year Anno di MCCC." There was also a Lady von Lichtenstein, buried in 1507, whose full-length portrait on her tombstone eyed me with drowsy curiosity, because the house in which I was born once had belonged to her. Thus surrounded with history, I was made into a Roman Catholic.

The priest poured warm Holy Water over my head, blew on me, used oils, and, bowing three times to the west, he exorcised the last lingering connections with sin. After Frau Schütz's beautiful navel, I now had been given a beautiful soul. "St. Boniface," the priest said, "will stand by him all his life as his guardian and defend his Catholic soul!" Although she never went to church, my mother got goose bumps when she heard these words and was seized by religious awe. She always said that she fainted at the moment of transubstantiation; she didn't know what it was, but the minute it turned quiet and the bells tinkled, everything went black, and therefore she stayed at home and worshiped God in her heart. My father looked uneasy and avoided looking at the priest. His SA uniform didn't look correct in the chapel, but he himself had nothing against baptisms because every child should have one. And besides, St. Boniface was a very respectable historical figure.

The dinner that followed my baptism is a matter of historical record. Witnesses recall me as a calm, bundled shape being handed around in a swell of food and drink: beef soup with dumplings, red and white cabbage, boiled potato dumplings, roast veal, smoked ham (cured in the Kuhns' own smokehouse), boiled celery salad, huge round loaves of freshly baked bread, dark beer from Bamberg, wine, champagne and plum schnapps. For dessert, Frau Kuhn served compote of prunes and apricots, then came a huge cake topped with a stork holding a baby in its beak. People were eating so earnestly that they lost interest in me, and I was put down on the Kuhns' old Biedermeier sofa under a sweet-looking madonna that cuddled Jesus in her arms.

While the guests wiped the sweat off their faces, they began to talk politics. My mother clearly remembers that tiny, fox-eyed Herr Kuhn, who had drunk too much of his own illegally brewed schnapps, said that all the talk about German blood and soil and the sacred German Farmer was *"Scheissdreck"*— shit-turds — and made up by poets who didn't know anything about farming; they didn't know a pig's turd from a cow's; and as far as he was concerned, the expense of the *Reichsparteitage* in Nürnberg wasn't worth horseshit; the party bosses could all kiss his ass...

Frau Kuhn said that this was nice talk for a baptism! And my godfather, who had held me in his black SS-uniform at the altar and had sworn to be a guiding influence on my future life, got up and said that he couldn't tolerate such talk at his godson's baptism. Germany was going through a glorious revolutionary phase that cleansed us of past indignities and prepared a noble future for such as me. Pointing in my direction, he said I was still an unwritten book, full of pure pages in which German history would write its chapters. My mother rose at this point and proposed a toast to me, bringing the argument to an end.

But my baptism wasn't over yet; people continued to bring presents, tributes to the gendarme's son. My mother kept a record (written on the reverse side of the bill for the dining room set they had bought on the installment plan at a large furniture store in Bamberg) of the presents that I had received: a long chain of small smoked link sausages; a small cured ham; a bottle of plum schnapps; several blue baby hats that the ladies from my mother's National Socialist Women's Club had hand knitted themselves, with Germanic runes embroidered on them; a plastic blue bib; a bowl of ripe yellow pears; a cartload of firewood; a stoneware plate with the portrait of Adolf Hitler on it (from my godfather and his wife who headed the local BDM Chapter); a small crystal beer mug with a silver rim and the engraved inscription: 'Winfried-1937'; a leather-bound catechism with colorful pictures (from the Kuhns); a cheap *History of Aviation* (a present from the Kuhns' youngest son who had just joined the Hitler Youth and started to fly gliders in the Rhön Mountains) that showed aviators in leather outfits beside their flying machines, casually smoking cigarettes; and a little book which my sister Gertrude had made for me. She had stitched ten sheets of paper together with black thread and put a transfer picture on the front: a little shepherdess and a little shepherd in a field of blue forget-me-nots, surrounded by fluffy white sheep. Underneath, Gertrude had written in the stiff, formal script of an eight-year-old: "*Tagebuch*, diary, Winfried November 10,1937." And, underneath that, assuming my own identity, she wrote: "*Mein Leben*, my life," as if she saw my life ahead of her surrounded by fragrant meadows of forget-me-nots. Later on I always assumed that the shepherdess in the picture was Gertrude, and the shepherd I, and that we lived a secret second life in a safe and beautiful blue-hazy realm in the midst of luxurious grass and flowers on a plane other than the one we knew.

There was also a little religious pamphlet on the life of St. Boniface (a present from the old maid who took care of the Kuhns' kitchen), showing the saint with a gaunt face and his arms stretched toward heaven on the front cover, his head encircled by a radiant halo which gave him an otherworldliness. It was called *A Brief Sketch of St. Boniface's Martyrdom* and underneath the subtitle in small print said: "Suffering leads to God." The old maid who had given me the booklet didn't have a proper name. Everybody called her "*Die Patin*," the godmother, because she had led someone's child at baptism, but it had been so long ago that nobody remembered that *Die Patin* came late because she had gone to St. Kilian's to ask the priest to bless her gift for me. She wanted me to be saintly from the start. She put the book on St. Boniface next to my face and the saint's image went straight into my wide-open eyes (which were still blue, as is often the case with newborn children), and I developed a strong partiality for the suffering of St. Boniface as I grew up.

I had the text read to me and I looked at the colorful illustrations tracking the saint's travels across heathen Germany. A picture toward the end of the book especially captivated my imagination. It showed the saint in the Germans' brutal hands while they were raising their clubs to smash his head and body. Frau Kuhn always pointed to the saint whom she called "my divine self," meaning me, and said: "Look! How the poor saint is suffering for Heaven!" She called the pagans evil but the word didn't make an impression on me. I looked at the wild pagans from St. Boniface's position with excited anticipation. That was the difference between me and the saint: he looked upward, into Heaven, I looked at the pagans' ferocious bodies which the artist had made very three-dimensional with sinews and muscles that strained under their long flying blond hair. They had wide-open mouths exposing strong teeth in perfectly harmonious scale with their naked limbs, and had come out of the dense green forests that were always in the background. After I had imagined

21

the martyrdom of St. Boniface, I would wander off with the
pagans into the woods.

After the Patin's gift my mother made only one more entry on her list. It was the midwife Frau Schütz's present.
Hers was the most impressive of them all, truly spectacular.
She brought a four-foot spiced blood sausage that not only
had been born on the same day as I but also weighed the
same. The spiced sausage closed my mother's list. The world
had come to my cradle to wish me well and to launch me on
my way! My mother folded the bill of sale in half and tucked
it in her memory album next to a pressed cowslip she had
picked years before in a meadow under the Castle Bant.

≋ 3 ≋

F rau Schütz's blood sausage, my soulless twin, also born
in steam and turmoil under the sign of Scorpio,
quickly vanished in the digestive juices of my family.
I, on the other hand, grew bigger and started to develop more
focused features.

My first photograph shows me on my back, my legs in
the air, all in white from top to bottom, with pompoms sticking up from a white woolen hat. I appear absolutely rigid on
a rug in the Kuhns' garden. It must have been a sunny day
some time in early spring, 1938. And then another photo
from around the same time — me in my mother's arms. I'm
looking straight into her face. My mother is wearing a long
plaid skirt down to her ankles and her hair is pulled back
into a bun. Aryan mother holding Aryan son. That's what all
her friends from the NS-Frauenschaft looked like that year.

My mother, busy with me, had given up recruiting women for the National Socialist Women's Club that year. She belonged all to me.

My father took the picture. His shadow is visible in the foreground, as always. In the background beyond the Kuhns' fence is a small cottage, and next to it a large magnificent Franconian half-timbered barn — neat, well-kept, solid, and German. Behind the barn is a brick house with shutters, and next to it a large swastika on a tall pole. It must have been a holiday, maybe April 20, Hitler's birthday. He celebrated his forty-ninth that year.

Motherhood, babyhood, fatherhood (though invisible, managing the camera), and Agfahood 1938. We are all together in this one. With a little click the camera placed me permanently in my mother's arms. The Kuhns' cherry and apple trees will wait for all eternity for their leaves to unfold. History looks, as a swastika, like a half-closed eye, from across the stone wall.

Shortly afterward Hitler marched into the Sudetenland while Chamberlain waved a piece of paper in the cold winds at the London airport, my parents worried about me because my hair didn't grow the way it was supposed to grow. I still had the same silky baby-blonde hair (with a touch toward the brown spectrum) which I had at birth. They massaged my head, but nothing became of it. They tried lotions, in vain. They rubbed chamomile and wormwood tea into my scalp. Nothing. An old farmhand of the Kuhns suggested fresh horse dung, but my parents said they would wait. And then my mother talked to Frau Schütz of the impeccable navels; and she knew the answer. My hair should be cut down to the roots, several times in a row, and then it would be stimulated to grow. The local barber came to our house and shaved off my hair with a razor while my father held my head. The entire household stood around and watched my baby hair float to the ground, while my mother gathered strands and tucked them into an envelope.

The bald period in my life is well-documented by an over active Agfa. A series of Winfried-our-little-boy-without-hair snapshots show me lying on my stomach, on my back, propped up by women in white clothes, and I'm always on the same rug in the garden. The trees have thick foliage, the grass is sprinkled with dandelions; spring and summer had come to Franconia while the barber came every week to shave off the slightest show of fuzzy hair.

●　　●　　●

History came to us in Pfarrweisach over our new *Telefunken*. During the same period when my parents over-saw the weekly visits of the barber, my father had bought a big new radio on the installment plan. Frau Kuhn said that it was as big as a small rowboat. The *Telefunken* had all the latest gadgets, even a green cat's eye, which opened and closed to show how finely the stations were tuned.

As soon as the tubes had warmed up, news arrived in Pfarrweisach. While being informed of Germany's latest con-quests, my mother knitted, my father read the papers, and my sisters did their homework. My parents shook their heads while listening to the announcer of the *Deutschlandsender* and went back to worrying about my baldness. I was bigger than history. I loomed larger in their future than the conquest of Austria and the Sudetenland. It was clear that Czechoslova-kia would be next, but they couldn't do anything about for-eign countries. They could do something about my hair. I was all they wanted from history. Further, my first birthday was coming up. The year had come full circle and the sun was rising in Scorpio again. Frau Schütz slaughtered a fat sow as usual, to get her through the winter, and Pfarrweisach had another *Kermesse*.

• • •

November 10, 1938. History even gave it a name: *Kristallnacht*. On November 9, a few fours before the heavens recreated the constellations that they had had at my birth a year before, the Germans started to burn synagogues, smash Jewish shops, beat up Jews, kill them, and wrote *"Juden Raus!"* on walls all over Germany; they made big bonfires of Jewish loot that lasted far into my birthday. My second year was ushered in by a wild national celebration, but I wasn't conscious of it. I was cozily bundled in my eiderdown comforter in my bed next to my parents. There were no Jews in Pfarrweisach and so everything was quiet. Our *Telefunken* said the next day that Germans, infuriated by Zionist conspiracies, had taken the law into their own hands and had spontaneously given vent to their frustration.

While the November skies still smoked over Germany, I had a birthday cake with one candle. My father bought me a wooden horse with a bushy white tail. I also got a new winter outfit, and Frau Schütz brought a *Lebkuchenherz* from one for the booths on the market square. Everybody commented on how big and strong I had grown; they patted my bald head and said that I looked like a real strong Franconian boy, a real little National Socialist!

On my first birthday it looked like I would need all my ancestral vitality and my Aryan robustness to cope with the strain of helping rule the world! I was exactly four months and a day old when we had gotten Austria back; one year, four months, and a day when the Czechs came home into the Reich (Czechoslovakia was practically a Franconian province now); I wasn't even two years old when Poland collapsed. I was only one day short of two and a half when we marched into Norway and Denmark, and for the next two years it went like a flu epidemic; the Netherlands in five days, Belgium in eighteen, Greece in fifteen, and Yugoslavia in eleven. I was dizzy and had to rest in the Kuhns' garden on my woolen blanket, looking at the dandelions, filling my eyes with dark shades of green, which is very calming. It must have been after the fall of Paris in June of 1940 that somebody decided that I had to celebrate our victories. I am sitting all in white on a chair in the middle of the Kuhns' garden. The Agfa shot is slightly blurred, because I was moving around. I am drinking out of a huge beer mug, my head bent back as if I were trying to get the last drop. All around me is lush summer vegetation.

§ 4 §

I n my first recorded memory, I see a nurse dressed in white moving across the room to take me out of my mother's arms. The nurse is wearing a reddish-brown button over her big left breast; she puts me on a scale suspended from a hook. I'm being weighed; I'm softly bouncing up and down. That's the end of this vision, which my mother always said I must have dreamed up because she couldn't remember anything like it. But there are two more memories from that warm and cuddled period of my life — it's a triptych. As soon as one panel comes into view the other two unfold automatically.

A tall woman in a blue apron is carrying me downstairs in the Kuhns' house. I'm on her right arm. She is opening the front door that has big wide steps leading down into the court. Others are already in front of the door. They look into the night sky. The woman points upward, saying: "Look, look! Zeppelin!" I'm looking upwards in the direction of the noise of whirring motors. A huge, dark, cigar-shaped mass with flashing red and white lights appears. Everybody shouts as the dirigible moves across the sky. The outstretched left arm of the woman that carries me moves with the aircraft and then slowly descends.

The third panel has the most colors. My mother, a young man, and I (holding onto my mother's right arm) are walking along a wooden fence in a green meadow. Brown cows graze on the other side. My mother talks to the man who has dark hair and tanned-looking skin. His face has pockmarks and small eruptions. I let go of my mother and stretch out my arms to the man. He picks me up and as soon as my face is at the level of his, I am flinging my arms around his neck and I kiss him on his cheek. I won't let go, the man laughs, and my mother pulls me away with force. She's saying, *"Was den Kindern manchmal einfällt…!"* "the things children do…" My mother is embarrassed. My memory lapses; but there's an epilogue. My mother pulls out her handkerchief, wets it with her saliva, and wipes my mouth. She scrubs hard, saying "Don't go around kissing strangers. They can have a disease!"

The word *mirabellen* is one of my first verbal memories.

The plums came with summer. Red, but more yellow than red, my mother put them on top of cakes with a clear glaze over them. My mother said: "Today we are going to pick *mirabellen* in the Kuhns' garden!" Her tongue glided over the word as if she were sucking it. Her saliva gave the word juice. I put the tiny plums in my mouth without eating them. I fondled them with my tongue before I bit into the flesh which resisted the teeth at first, then squirted sweet juice to the roof of my mouth.

While my tongue searched out *mirabellen* in the Kuhns' big garden our *Telefunken* announced the big world outside. Warsaw had fallen. A snapshot shows me sitting on a swing in a daisied garden. I'm swinging right into the Franconian sky leaving the daisies behind. The next shot on the Agfa-Lupex film captured the black announcement box that the SS had put up on the walls of the gendarmerie. The box is between two windows that have small lacy curtains. Behind large-meshed chicken wire are the latest bulletins of September 1939. The camera was close enough for the headlines: Warsaw about to fall! And there is a series of photographs of German generals, and a large poster with the inscription "Hitler and Europe." On top of the black wood is the SS insignia in white and the name THE BLACK CORPS — Gendarmerie Pfarrweisach.

I lived one floor above the SS box and developed definite personality traits that entertained all the neighbors, who poetically called me *ein kleines Donnerwetter,* "a little thunderhead." I had developed a fascination for our cleaning woman, a widow in long black skirts, who came once a week on Fridays to scrub our floors. While she was kneeling on the floor, I crept up from behind and dumped her bucket of rinsing water. Her long skirts were soaked. I wouldn't listen to reason; nothing could stop me from dumping the water on the floor while the old widow screamed "Jesus and Mary!" and crossed herself. My mother had to lock the rooms where she cleaned, because the widow said she wouldn't come anymore — her wet skirts gave her rheumatism. Shut off from the black widow, I turned to our chamber pots. Since the toilet was at the end of a long dark corridor, we used chamber pots as did everyone in Pfarrweisach. Sometime between the fall of Warsaw and the surrender of Paris, I started to get to our full pots in the morning and dump them over the floors. It made my mother frantic and the neighbors laugh. My mother had to clear away the pots before I rose.

And then, one day in spring 1940, while Germany prepared for the invasion of the British Isles, I disappeared. I had run past blooming apple and apricot trees to the little train station where long red diesel trains arrived from Bamberg. My mother caught me just as I was climbing into the train. I had my little toy brown suitcase in one hand and my oilcloth from my bed neatly folded over my arm. Asked why I had taken the sheet along (it smelled of rubber and recent bed-wetting), I responded that this was my raincoat. Nobody traveled without one.

•   •   •

France had surrendered — our *Telefunken* said so. Summer 1940. We went on long walks every Sunday afternoon, my mother in organdy dress, my father in suit and tie with the party button on his lapel, my sisters in light summer dresses. During one of our outings, my father shot the most successful childhood picture of me. It was blown up and my mother put it on her night table.

I'm standing in a field of grass and clover. Some of the plants are so high they reach to my shoulders. At my back are two apple trees, slightly out of focus. My knees show round and pudgy in my short pants, held up by white suspenders with edelweiss embroidered on them. My pants have an embroidered flap up front, easy to unbutton whenever I had to take a leak. Somebody had put the SS insignia on the flap. Sharp and angular, the emblem looks like two flashing thunderbolts. All is innocence and sun. Cirrus-blue summer clouds move above, and I am smiling radiantly into the camera, holding a daisy. One is tempted to kiss my healthy cheeks, grown fat on Franconian milk and sausages. The shavings have paid off: I have a full shock of dark blonde hair that flops down over my forehead. Every time my hair is washed, my mother rinses it with a rosemary extract. It shines in the summer sun.

•   •   •

There are endless pictures of this period that show us in forests and fields in and around Pfarrweisach. Germany stretched from Poland to the French Atlantic. Her borders were secure; the south was protected by our ally Mussolini. We were right in the center of things, surrounded by alfalfa fields, wheat, and rye. My mother loved to have her picture taken standing in a wheat field looking at the heavy stalks as if she were an agricultural inspector giving her opinion on the crop's quality. We are around her squinting in the sun, waiting for the shutter to click. The settings change but the poses remain: summery dresses, bouquets of wildflowers, rustic benches under oak trees, an outing that ended on a terrace of a *Gasthaus* called Waldesruh, drinking lemonade

and eating cake. I can still smell the heat of July while floating on my father's shoulders down a narrow country lane.
Poppies are growing in the wheat — red, velvety, the black of
the stamen comes off, like tulips. Down the road is a red
church steeple and yellow wheat fields. My father points out
larks that rise straight into a blue sky. He pretends he is a
horse, I the rider, and we gallop down the road into the watery summer heat to the spot where a lark is hovering.

▨ 5 ▧

That year I was a happy boy. Stories underscore that
summer like background music to the backdrop of
alfalfa and clover fields. For example, the Kuhns took
in two German soldiers who had been wounded in France.
While recuperating, they helped in the fields where my mother
and sisters worked too. My mother flirted with the soldiers;
they pelted each other with flowers and chased around the
bundled wheat. In the evening my mother put thistles into
their beds. The soldiers slept in the nude and had to use
pincers to get the thorns out. Screams and laughter at the
Kuhns' rang out all night long. When they left, they brought
my mother a bouquet of roses with thistles hidden in it.
Laughter and farewell tears followed. My mother said, *"Ach,
das war eine schöne Zeit, so was kommt nicht wieder...!"* For the
adults, Pfarrweisach was a green memory in which happiness glowed like ripe yellow apples, which they picked whenever they became sad. They devoured the fragrant fruit with
glittering eyes that became moist as they chewed the past.

In October 1940, just when Hitler decided to postpone the invasion of England, my father was promoted to Meister of the gendarmerie. We received another heavy piece of parchment signed by the president of the German Gendarmerie and by Hitler (in proxy, of course) under an eagle with a swastika, saying that my father had been promoted in the name of the Führer and Volk, and that we had been transferred to Kitzingen, a town on the Main River.

While Hitler was eyeing the conquest of Russia, I had to leave Pfarrweisach, the womb of my umbilical cord. I wore my good black velvet suit with the short pants as the gates of Pfarrweisach closed behind me. I lost Frau Schütz whom I never saw again. She died one day in 1952 while making sausages. My mother said it was a good death, a real Frau-Schütz-death, always in the midst of things. But back in October 1940, Frau Schütz had no thoughts about dying and was cutting star-shaped navels throughout northern Franconia. She came to our house before we left and brought me a picture of St. Boniface. In the little picture, he is fighting off attacking pagans with a bishop's staff; Frau Schütz said that the Bishop of Bamberg had blessed the picture and it would help me ward off evil. My mother saved it for me and put it into her memory album where it took on the smell of her past.

• • •

"Heaven is crying because you're leaving," Frau Kuhn said as we left Pfarrweisach. It was raining and the whole neighborhood stood in front of the gendarmerie and saw us off. Although I don't remember that part of the story, I recall other things. Our move must have shaken my not-yet-three-year-old psyche; I was displaced; in the middle of upheaval. My escape to the station at two-and-a-half shows that traveling was running in my genes. Maybe it was handed down from the roving robber barons, or from my maternal grandfather who had only come one October day in 1940. I remember that we rode with the movers. My father had gone ahead by car and we sat in a passenger cabin in a van hitched to a moving truck. Everything we owned fitted into the two vans. The cabin in front of the van came to a round point. It looked like the gondola of a zeppelin. I sat on a stiff seat and watched the rainy Franconian landscape move by. My mother wore her best black suit and a black hat with a spotted veil across her face. When she spoke, the veil moved with her breath. It made me think of spiders crawling in a web.

· · ·

I'm standing in a fine cold drizzle, in the way of the movers; I feel displaced. The dimensions are bigger than the ones I am used to. Colors are duller and smaller. No green spaces. I walk up a small cobblestone, dead end street in front of our new home. A big brown gate with rusting hinges is at the end of the little hill, a large lock is at the level of my eyes. I am looking through the keyhole; there is an orchard in the rain on the other side. A strong draft is whistling through the keyhole, and the lock smells like oil and wet rust. I am tiny. I am cold. I am overcome by rainy drafts. Our new house is painted an old flaky yellow. Unlike the Kuhn's house, our new house looks at me with indifference. It doesn't know me, its walls shut their eyes and don't invite me to come inside. But I have to enter, it's the only warm place.

• • •

We moved into an old Benedictine monastery where our apartment was on the second floor next to my father's office. The walls of the abandoned monastery were a meter thick and our apartment was so cold that the water in the pitchers on the bedroom dressing tables froze during the following December, while our radio announced that the Axis powers had signed their agreement in Berlin. My sisters slept in the old refectory with ceilings over twenty feet high. Gertrude was afraid of ghosts and she infected me with stories about the big hole in the garden next door below our windows. It was the opening to a secret passage that connected the Benedictines with a nunnery up the hill. The monks used the passage to drag off their victims. They let them die there and the tunnel was full of skeletons. At night when I was safe and warm in my bed next to my parents' bed, I thought of gray shapes in black holes. I didn't dare move for fear I might attract the dead monks' attention below. A year after we moved in, the tunnel was filled in; the dead monks vanished with the closing of the open hole.

After Pfarrweisach, Kitzingen was immense. Gertrude took me up to the attic and showed me the sights. She wagged her index finger at me and pointed in different directions. I followed her finger across the red tile roofs of Kitzingen dotted with church spires. There was a river called Main that divided the town from a suburb called Etwashausen, meaning something sticking out. Vineyards grew along the river, and Kitzingen had industry. There was an airfield in the east and large barracks in the west. And it would take us much longer now to reach *"die Natur"* for our Sunday walks. She pointed to a tall medieval tower with a leaning hood. Gertrude said that it was crooked because they had mixed wine into the cement during a drought year. And Kitzingen had four churches: St. Johannis, St. Petrini, the Balthasar Neumann Kirche, and St. Mary's. My eyes followed her finger to the new unusual shapes, so different from St. Kilian's where the priest had blown his breath up my nostrils to open the passage for my Christian soul to breathe.

• • •

Our monastery had two wings joined like a big L. The gendarmerie was in one, and Mr. and Mrs. Beyer lived in the empty wing that had been a federal tax office. And the garden behind the house was divided into two parts: the Beyers' and ours. The Beyers grew crabgrass and flowers, and we, along with the other three families in the gendarmerie, grew vegetables.

The daisies and the dandelions of Pfarrweisach were lost forever. There were no seed pods that flew through the summer air in our new garden. It was a garden neatly parceled out: the lieutenant who was above my father had more than we had; and we had more than the other two families, because we were second in command. We had a raspberry patch and red grapes that grew on a trellis on the back of the house right up to the third floor. The trunks had been planted by the monks and the vines were gnarled and hairy-looking. They wound themselves around the office window where the gendarmes sat behind their telephones and typewriters. In the spring the vines unfurled tiny leaves and whitish buds. In the summer the leaves nearly covered the office window from where the blue cigarette smoke of the gendarmes curled lazily into the blue air.

The Kuhns' garden had no boundaries. It went off into infinity, a succession of greens and blues, darks and lights. In Kitzingen, our garden was finite and defined. Here were our cabbages, there theirs. The lieutenant had a garden of his own, fourteen steps above ours. Lilacs and chestnuts bloomed in the spring. Even the pear tree in the middle of the garden was divided among the gendarmes. We had one fourth of it. Sometime in 1941, a gendarme stuck an old wardrobe into the tree and said that it was my tree house. When I climbed into it, I could hear the gendarmes speaking in the office and could smell their cigarette smoke.

• • •

Our garden was bordered in the south by a high wall separating us from the municipal hospital. Its operating room was on the same level as our bedrooms. It had ordinary glass in the windows and my mother discovered hemorrhoid operations. She said they were more dramatic than other operations. She got out my father's field glasses and watched from behind our curtains. She got neighbors to watch with her. One day she called Frau Nüsslein, the lieutenant's wife. I stood behind the two women as they passed the heavy hunting glasses back and forth. I asked to have a look, and they put me on a chair and Frau Nüsslein held the glasses in front of my eyes. They needed adjusting, but finally I saw white figures around a table under a big light. My mother said that the patient had his rear end sticking up into the air; customary for hemorrhoids. My mother said that they were something people had in the back and it hurt. Frau Nüsslein told me that the dark spot in the middle of the white sheet was hemorrhoids.

Hemorrhoids rang in my ears and floated before my eyes while Germany overran Yugoslavia and Greece in the early spring of 1941. I told my neighborhood friends that we watched hemorrhoid operations. They wanted to watch, too, and so one day while my mother had the field glasses out again, I ran downstairs and brought up the neighbors' children. My mother stared at us with a red face and said that children were not allowed to watch operations. Only adults had hemorrhoids and children had nothing to do with them. It increased the mystery. Doctors' hands were drawn to a dark spot in the middle of a raised white shape. They put things in and took things out. It was a funny and painful ritual, ambiguous, mysterious. I was drawn to the window and watched distant figures with gloved hands converging on a dark center, passive and expectant. I watched with questions on my mind, but answers never came. The hospital must have noticed the reflections of field glasses on our side of the garden and put in frosted glass.

•   •   •

Nineteen forty one was a big year for Germany. We swept through north Africa. Our *Telefunken* reported one big news event after another. While the tubes glowed with an orange light and the cat's eye quivered when we had static, the loud speaker announced that President Roosevelt had signed the lend-lease laws; but Germany was able to cope with it.

I played on the Landwehrplatz on the north end of our house. The square was an oval-shaped park without grass. A granite slab elevated the tightly packed soil from the asphalt of the Landwehrstasse. Nothing sprouted on the clay soil, and whenever it rained the ground was covered with a slippery, slimy-looking film. From the ground fifteen large linden trees grew upwards. Their crowns stuck together and in the summer the sun filtered through the green leaves in big irregular patches. The square gave an illusion of green spaces, but it was no comparison to the lost fields of Pfarrweisach.

• • •

Hitler and Göring hung on the east wall of our big entrance hall with the gothic arches — two color photographs, framed and under glass. A crest of laurels with the words "Gendarmerie Kitzingen" hung between them. Every time I left the house or entered, Hitler and Göring were in their proper places surrounded by the smell of waxed floors and humid, whitewashed walls. Both wore brown uniforms with capes flung backwards. A leather strap ran across Hitler's chest. Göring had his left hand resting against his hip, Hitler his right. Göring held a marshal's baton in his right hand. "Like a fat little emperor," a friend of my mother once said as they came down the staircase. "Shhh!" my mother said, putting her index finger across her lips.

Göring looked to the left, Hitler to the right. But their eyes did not meet. Their glances wandered off into infinity. Maybe their eyes intersected each other on some unknown plane. I stood in front of the photographs and looked at them sideways to see if I could follow the direction of their eyes. I stood right underneath them, touching the wall and looked upwards; but I saw nothing. I asked if they could see me; my parents laughed. But one of the gendarmes said that the *Führer* and the *Reichsmarshall* were there to make sure that I hung out the big swastika on holidays. Every time a national holiday came around I asked my father if we would put out the flag. We hoisted the bright red and black swastika on the flagpole that was set in the yellow wall of the old monastery right over the main entrance. In the breeze the swastika sounded like water lapping against a beach. If there was no wind the swastika was hidden in folds of the cloth. At night I could hear the flag move outside. The pole creaked softly and the rope hit the wood with gentle thuds. Back in Pfarrweisach Mr. Kuhn, who had joined the SS to go horseback riding, was drafted and made a guard at the concentration camp Oranienburg. Mrs. Kuhn wrote my mother to complain about it, saying that her husband had nothing to do with the SS and politics, he just wanted to go horseback riding in the club. It was a terrible world compared to what it was when we still lived in Pfarrweisach.

◈ 6 ◈

Jews were ghosts. I had never seen any, but they existed because people talked about them. The word "Jude" came out of their mouths unlike other words. It wasn't a neutral word. People said *"Jude," "Jüdin,"* or *"Juden,"* with a particular tone in their voices. They charged the words with colors that they didn't give other words. "Jew" always insinuated things; it produced undulating waves of hidden emotions. When people told stories about Jews, my ears picked up on the unsaid things: repulsive, dark, dirty, dangerous, funny, mocking, comical, alien, and sad. Sometimes people said *"Jüddel,"* or *"Jid,"* instead of *"Jude"* and that gave the personae in the stories a funny, belittled character right from the start — a Jew was a comical aside. And the accent on the word *"Jude"* seemed to be stronger than on other words, ordinary words. There was nothing ordinary in *"Jude."* The vowel was stretched into infinity; the long "u" in *"Jude"* threw off the smell of garlic and raw onions, because Jews ate both of them all the time. A Jew smelled; so did the word.

Pfarrweisach didn't have any Jews. But Kitzingen had a Jewish history, especially around the Landwehrplatz. At the north end of the linden trees was the shell of a big synagogue with two towers. It was boarded up. It had burned during the *Kristallnacht* while I, cuddled in warm blankets in my bed in Pfarrweisach, had peacefully slept into my first birthday. And across from the Beyers' section of our old monastery was an abandoned red building with gothic windows that looked like blind eyes onto the Landwehrstrasse. My parents told me that they didn't know what it was, but a neighbor said it was a Jewish school; it had been closed a few years back. "You should have heard the noise they made in there," she said. She started to imitate the noise: she clucked like a hen and revolved her tongue in her open mouth. It sounded as if she had an apple in her mouth while unfamiliar sounds rose and fell: Jewish children learning Hebrew, an alien language. *"Hebräisch"* sounded in the neighbor's mouth like something that should be flushed down the toilet.

Before my eyes Jews and Jewesses crystallized: ghosts made up of the same qualities that people had in the tone of their voices and attached to the characters in their stories.

Aunt Anna came for a visit. Everyone sat around the living room table and drank coffee while she told a story: when she was young, Jews lived across the street from her. One of the men always urinated in the garden instead of going into the outhouse. He stood there with his hands behind his head while he urinated *"im hohen Bogen,"* in a wide arch across the garden... *"jüdisch, ro richtig jüdisch! Solche Schweine!"* Also *"sowas!"* They shook their heads and sipped from their cups.

Someone told another story. The Jews in their town belonged to a special sect. If one of them was ill for more than eight days, the rabbi came and broke his neck. The neighbor who told the story cracked her knuckles to imitate the sound. They weren't allowed to be sick over the Sabbath, she said. And when they were buried the people following the coffin threw stones to chase away Jesus! Everyone stared at the woman who told the story. *"So was!"* they said, and shook their heads.

Tante Anna said that one of the Jewesses living across the road from her always took some work with her when she went to the outhouse. She even would take a bowl of dough with her. She kneaded the dough into submission. Pale dough reminded me of unwashed hands. Jews had pale, unwashed hands. Jews were connected with toilets, urination, and defecation. And then one day, while I pretended I was playing in a corner while the adults spoke to each other in low voices, I heard them say that the German army in Czechoslovakia had captured a nest of Jews who had kidnapped and killed little Christian boys and girls and used their blood in baking matzos. They said they had found the small carcasses in a kosher butcher shop hanging from hooks like pigs and cows. I was a little Christian boy.

To the color of defiled, pale dough came the burst of blood and terror. Jews and Jewesses smelling like garlic chased little boys down the road. I was one of them. I was terrified and fascinated. Sometimes I was captured. My imagination

41

stopped in a white butcher's shop with gleaming hooks, like the shop where my mother bought her meat. Dark, bearded and hairy men with big noses overpowered me. Jews.

•   •   •

While Germany invaded Russia and while Churchill and Roosevelt met on the Atlantic, my mind assembled from various elements what my ears had extracted from the adults' conversations — lurid scenes of terror over and over again. I was always on the verge of being captured by dark hairy Jews who wanted to hang me from a hook. It never got to that point because I always started the Jewish chase from the beginning at that point. While I played the tiny Christian child pursued by dark aliens, the external world went on as usual. Nobody suspected that I was pursued by imaginary Jews.

Frau Lachmann, who lived in the green house across the street, arrived every morning with her milk cart. She sold skimmed milk and regular milk for money and ration coupons. She always wore pulse warmers. My mother said she had cold blood. She held the milk pails with strong bony hands as if she wanted to strangle them. In the winter, big white clouds issued from her mouth as she ladled the milk from her shiny cans into our milk pail in the frosty air.

On the other side of our garden Herr Beyer watered his nasturtiums and potted oleander plants. He had a fat stomach and looked like one of the kings in Grimm's *Fairy Tales*. He murmured to himself as he carefully examined each flower and picked snails which he threw into a bucket of water to drown.

Everything had its color, shape and smells. The laundry

on the way to the garden smelled like *Kernseife* and scrubbed tin tubs. The grey, worn wooden paddles for beating the laundry stood neatly arranged according to size in the corner. The color of the fence that divided our garden from the Beyers' was worn and washed out, rotting under years of rain. The stairs to the downstairs hall were gleaming with wax; I knew every step and turn by heart. As soon as I reached the last step, I confronted Hitler and Göring on the wall, stern and distant.

While our armies stormed into Russia and landed in north Africa, Frau Beyer shook her mop from one of the upstairs windows every morning, my mother beat her rugs clean in the garden with a rug beater, they both alternated waxing the staircases, and the blue smoke of the gendarmes curled from the office window.

Once in a while I visited my father in the office; he took me on his knees and let me type. He smelled like cigarette smoke. Over his desk was another photograph of Hitler, sepia-colored, his hair slicked down. Behind me in a cupboard were nightsticks, guns, and revolvers. The other gendarmes patted me on the head and said, *"Na, wie geht's Winfried?"* When the lieutenant came in, I stood up and shook hands with him, making a deep bow, a *"Diener."* *"Mach'n schönen Diener,"* my mother always told, because the lieutenant was above us in rank. His wife gave me a chocolate bar once in a while. I made bows clear down to the floor, and she always exclaimed, "What a polite little boy!"

Germany was at the peak of her power. The gendarmes had a big map of Europe and Africa on the wall; they had used red ink to shade in the territories that Germany held. The whole world was shaded red.

Our *Telefunken* announced Pearl Harbor a day after St. Nicholas had brought me apples and candy in his large bag. *"Ach Gott!"* my mother said to neighbors, "Where will it all end?" But everybody said that one or two more enemies wouldn't matter; the Americans had a bad army and they were all cowards. In the gendarmerie everything went on as usual.

A snapshot of the winter 1941-42 shows me standing on the Neue Brücke, the big bridge at the end of our block over which the federal highway 8 rolled. I'm in winter clothes, scarf, gloves, and woolen hat, holding onto a big German shepherd. I'm rosy and healthy. The river below is frozen, and the shadow of my father who took the picture is thrown by the winter sun in a sharp angle to the right of me. In the early spring of 1942, he took another shot of me, my mother, and my sister Gertrude. We are on the riverbanks, the bridge in the back of us; my mother is wearing a huge fox stole and a rakish hat pulled over her left side. The shadow of my father is again visible in the picture, this time on the wild grass of the embankment. We're all smiling: Sunday afternoon — we went home after our walk and had coffee and cake. The river is swollen with spring water, and I look like a happy dumpling living securely in the very center of the red-shaded area of the gendarmes' map.

•　•　•

Germany was at her zenith. While we prepared the second offensive against Russia, the first leaves of the

Landwehrplatz came out on the chestnut trees next to the empty Jewish school. First their branches grew dark brown, sticky buds at the ends that kept swelling up, secreting clear drops, like tiny beads of sugary sweat, until they burst and released soft, green leaves that unfurled for several days, giving the square the soft, green glow of young salad leaves that grew in my mother's vegetable bed.

After the leaves, the blossoms started to grow in small candelabras, white, with small tongues of red on the inside. Then, the linden trees unrolled their leaves: small, heart-shaped, dark green, sticky, and rough on the grayish underside like the furry, green caterpillars that ate the cabbage leaves in our garden. The linden trees started to bloom.

The Landwehrplatz was a big cup of steaming linden tea. In the daytime the trees were big beehives, and in the evening we took walks through the scented air. My sisters and other girls had put ladders against the trees and picked the blossoms. Their voices drifted through the darkness; I chewed on the honeyed, sticky blossoms, and my mother did breathing exercises, saying that linden fragrance was good for the lungs.

•   •   •

The German Army opened its summer offensive in Russia; all went well. The *Telefunken* glowed during the evening news, and Gertrude said that this time we were going to get old Stalin, we were bombing Moscow. The linden blossoms were drying in linen bags in the pantry. Every time someone opened the door the kitchen was flooded with their scent. Lieutenant Nüsslein got into the black DKW of the gendarmerie and drove off one day. He had taken me a few times for a ride in the car. It was made completely of plastic and plywood and smelled of gasoline, stale cigarette smoke and rubber. Lieutanant Nüsslein didn't come back. They found his car parked on a lonely country road close to Repperndorf; he had died of a heart attack.

Fran Nüsslein, who was called Frau Lieutentant Nüsslein, had red eyes; we gave our condolences. We shook hands, I bowed. Frau Nüsslein gave me a chocolate bar. On the wrapper was a turbaned Moor carrying a bowl of fruit. Frau Nüsslein cried. I smelled the chocolate through the foil. I was afraid to eat it for several days because I thought some of Lieutenant Nüsslein's death had gone into it. They brought his body back to the gendarmerie where they put him in his bed for a day. They carried him in on a stretcher. It was Lieutenant Nüsslein in his green uniform; but he was dead-pale and his mouth had touched him and the chocolate bar. I couldn't eat it. The chocolate was connected with the pale uniformed shape and the half-open mouth on the stretcher. I saw two Lieutenant Nüssleins. The familiar one, driving the DKW and curtly saying *"Hiel Hitler,"* and the one that "died alone on a lonely road." He was the pale one. He didn't move. I couldn't understand him, he repulsed me, scared me. He was a decaying mystery-lying in his bed in the lieutenant's apartment. The foil of the chocolate was infected by the lifeless lieutenant. It took me several days before I cautiously broke off a rib of the chocolate bar.

•   •   •

Erwin Rommel had reached El Alamein; Gertrude said Germany was going to take Cairo soon. We found it on the gendarmes' map in the office. The red ink was at its gates.

Around that time Herr Kolb from across the street climbed into his pear tree to saw off a dead branch. He had a heart attack and fell out of the tree. His wife screamed for help. My father and another gendarme ran over. My mother and I sat in the kitchen and waited for my father to return. We were both very quiet and I had to think of Lieutenant Nüsslein again. Herr Kolb was dividing himself like the lieutenant.

When my father returned, my suspicion that death was something unclean was confirmed. My father had massaged Herr Kolb's chest; he and the other gendarme had done everything they knew from the police handbook on first aid. But Herr Kolb was dead.

My father stripped himself in front of the kitchen sink and started to wash himself. He lathered his chest, arms, and face. He had black hair on his chest. The hair under his armpits was long and soapy. He washed very carefully. He was washing out the dead Mr. Kolb. I hoped that my father would start his washing all over again. He flung handfuls of water into his face; he made funny sounds as he blew the water away from his mouth. My mother washed his back with a washcloth. I wanted to make sure that every part of his body was clean before I sat on his knees again. My father cupped his hands and brought handfuls of water to his armpits. The soap was rinsed out. His body was full with curly wet hair. My mother massaged him with the towel.

· · ·

Herr Kolb was lying in a coffin in his living room, his nose pointed sharply upwards. A fly was crawling over his lips. Frau Kolb chased the fly away with her handkerchief. My mother pushed me toward Frau Kolb and said: "Shake

47

hands, and tell her you are sorry Herr Kolb died." I stood in front of Frau Kolb and couldn't shake hands with her. The white curtains were drawn in front of the windows; I could see the outline of the red geraniums on the windowsills outside. It was hot in the room; I smelled vinegar — sharp, stringent, mixed in with the sweet smell of flowers. It gave me goose bumps. My mother gently pushed me toward Frau Kolb, but I wouldn't budge. Frau Kolb looked at me with hostility, and my mother apologized to her and said she didn't know what was wrong with me.

It was Herr Kolb's corpse; his solemnly displayed dead flesh made my hair stand on end. His wife had touched him therefore I couldn't touch her. I didn't want to be infected. My mother told me after the funeral that it smelled like vinegar in the room because the *Leichenfrau*, the woman who had washed the dead Herr Kolb, had washed him thoroughly in a solution of water and vinegar. After that I gagged every time I tasted vinegar in our salad.

• • •

Our armies reached the Caucasian Mountains in Russia. Soon all of north Africa would be German too. The *Telefunken* was lit with news every evening. German armies executed daring pincer movements in the African desert. My mother knitted, Gertrude did her homework, my father read Grimm's *Fairy Tales* to me, my older sister was at the BDM. Every Friday it was our turn to bathe in the big bathroom next to the office. The copper boiler made warm comfortable noises; my mother put in the wood, my father sometimes scrubbed my back with the sponge and splashed water at me. And every Monday afternoon my father gave review sessions on

traffic regulations downstairs in the big entrance hall to traffic violators. I sat in the back and watched him explain charts
of intersections and move toy cars and streetcars into various
positions. Hitler and Göring were hanging above my father
and looked past the crowds as if they merely tolerated their
presence. After the traffic sessions, my father took me for
rides on his green motorcycle. We rushed across the Neue
Brücke. I sat on the gas tank. The wind took my breath
away: I gasped, my father laughed. In a cloud of noise and
wind we raced through the air; the river down below and the
houses on the other side flew past us. I wanted to go on
forever, but my father said, "No, no! My little bird, we have to
go back home."

▧ 8 ▨

Herr Nüsslein was dead; his wife moved to the Adolf
Hitler Strasse under the big old chestnut trees next
to the railway station. The chocolate bar she had
given me was the last chocolate I would see for years! My
mother said that only people with high rank had connections to chocolate and other luxuries. I could visit Frau
Nüsslein in her new house and she would give me some
chocolate. We did visit her; I sat on an uncomfortable chair
and rocked back and forth. My mother talked about the war
with Frau Nüsslein, and asked about her dead husband. Frau
Nüsslein cried and I was bored. When we left, I waited for
the chocolate but Frau Nüsslein gave me an apple. I was so
dazed that I ran headfirst into one of the chestnut trees along

the Adolf Hitler Strasse. When my mother laughed, I started to cry with rage and dissappointment; I blamed my mother. After that I refused to come along to visit Frau Nüsslein.

After the Nüssleins left, another lieutenant moved into the gendarmerie. We moved upstairs into a large apartment in the converted attic. The huge roof of the old monastery wrapped itself around us like a warm and comfortable monk's skirt. We had regular-sized rooms and distributed the three plants we had brought from Pfarrweisach: the jade plant went into the corridor, the zimmerlinde in the living room, and the asparagus plant into the dining room. Gertude watered them and carried them downstairs once in a while to let them have some sun. She talked to them like little cats, "There, there," she said, "get lots of sun, it's good for you," and she blew off the dust that had collected on the leaves.

Our neighbors across the hall were Lieutenant Kluge and his wife. He was in the army and always away — first on the western front and then in hospitals because he had a *Bauchschuss*. A bullet had gone through his stomach and out again. Whenever I heard the word *Bauchschuss*, with a strong accent on the first and the second syllables, I saw a bullet (it was a French bullet, my mother had told me) go through a stomach, making a sound like the word schuss, snakelike, hissing, tearing into matter that looked like the stomach of a rabbit or a pig, because I had seen their stomachs. My mother spoke of Lieutenant Kluge's *Bauchschuss* only with a lowered voice and a solemn tone. *Bauchschuss* was just at the edge of death. It gave Frau Kluge a dramatic halo. I was afraid to look her straight in the eyes: a wife of a man with *Bauchschuss* inspired awe. When the neighbors talked about Herr Lieutenant Kluge's paleness there was something unsaid in their voices. Their talk reminded me of conversations about Jews where something also was always omitted in what was said. *"Bauchschuss!"* The word sat in the intestine, full of juices from the lower tract. It sat in the lower register of words that I knew. *Bauch* sucked things in, *schuss* spat them back out, and it was surrounded by slimy matter that had a vague resemblance to blood sausages.

Frau Kluge was tall and blond. Her hair was nearly white; she wore it tied back in a bun. She always wore light blouses embroidered with Viking motifs or jewelry shaped like Germanic runes. Frau Kluge had a little boy named Harald who was just a toddler and also had her white hair. Once in a while Harald came to visit me. Once, just after I had taken a nap, my mother had sat me down on the kitchen table. I looked morosely at Harald below. He suddenly put my left big toe in his mouth, clamped his teeth around it, and started to suck it. I looked at him in horror. My mother laughed and called Frau Kluge. Both women stood in the kitchen and laughed while Harald sucked my toe. I screamed; I looked at the two women in disbelief. Didn't they see that Harald was sucking my insides out through my big toe?

The Kluges were above us in rank. My mother hesitated to borrow something from Frau Kluge unless it was an emergency. In their conversations I could always hear that the Kluges were a notch above us. The Kluges' apartment was cleaner than ours, smelled better than ours, they simply were better than we. The Ritters, on the other hand, who had moved into our old apartment, were below us. Their apartment was not as clean as ours, it smelled less aired, the floors were not as shiny as ours — because Herr Ritter was not a Meister like my father.

Hitler and Göring kept watch over our house. The particular smells that each family let escape from behind their

doors into the hall floated down to the two colored photographs and out into the garden. Everything was in order.
Every afternoon everybody sat in the garden under the pear
tree and talked about the vegetables that were growing there,
and how the peasants hoarded food; then the whole household watered the garden. It was balmy outside and the war
in Russia and north Africa was far away. Blue smoke cuddled
its way out of the office window.

• • •

Montgomery and Römmel were facing each other in the
desert, and I was contemplating myself. I had fallen into a
new stage right after we moved upstairs. It started all in our
new bathroom. It was very isolated with a vestibule in front
and a separate door. Next to the bathroom was a large unused storage room. If both doors were closed, the bathroom
was like a cell of the lost Benedictines. I heard only the water
drop in the tank. I stared at the soundless flat-green walls
and then turned my gaze downwards.

Our toilet, like most German toilets, caught the released
waste in the white porcelain bowl. Unless the chain was
pulled, everything stayed right there where it had fallen out
of the lower internal regions. I was hypnotized by it; I stared.
I studied the corpses of cucumber seeds, tough peas, and
cherry pits (swallowed against all warnings) that had made
the mysterious voyage through the middle of me and emerged
at the other end — worn, half-vanished. From cucumber
seeds and cherry pits, I progressed to the larger phenomena.

The effluvia of my interior geography — darkest Asia,
Hindustan and Kurdistan, the mystic murky Amazon, rose
and swirled around me, intoxicating my young senses, mak-

ing me dizzy with myself. Forgetting the world outside, Hitler and Göring, Rommel and Montgomery, even our *Telefunken,* I looked down between my crotch into the bowl and saw cities of the plains, mountains, petrified forests, deserts, rivers, lush jungles, and steaming volcanoes, just born and still in the process of momentous upheavals. I was struck dumb by the enormity that took place down there. It came from me, the unseen me; it was a witness to my unknown internal regions. On cold days, I saw steam rise, and felt cold on the inside because I had the impression everything warm had left me. I looked and saw that I had been turned into brown porridge, or long irregular sausages, not too different from those Frau Schütz used to make in Pfarrweisach. I constantly expelled myself and yet remained the same. It felt good to expel oneself; half pain, half pleasure. As soon as I felt the other I knocking at the door, I ran to our secluded bathroom and let the spasm rip through my lower parts... it took my breath away: the other I poured out of me.

I made geography. I became my own atlas. I could create the same colors of plains and mountains that my sister Gertrude had in her school atlas. I found Kiev; I built a railroad line to Moscow; I bombed railways and viaducts, just like the Germans did, according to our *Telefunken*. My malleable self was endless in its variations. I created the entire war in it.

Sometimes I had intestinal worms. I expelled hot steaming worlds teeming with white wriggling worms, half-submerged, white and naked to the eye. I was hypnotized by the moving mass I had created. A part of me had appeared — alive. Contortive white corkscrews were twisting frantically in the dark matter. I had given birth to these white life forms, which were dangerous to my health, as I was always told.

They came if I didn't wash my hands, or ate carrots and other vegetables right out of the ground. They gave me dark circles under my eyes, they sapped my strength, they said. But in spite of it I loved my parasites. They were me, witness to my unseen insides. Sometimes I didn't tell my mother for a few days. They were messengers from me to me; mystical night creatures suddenly exposed to the light of day. I hesitated before I pulled the chain. Torrents of gurgling waters, making slurping sounds and giving the impression that the water couldn't wait to be sucked down the pipe, flushed the white worms into oblivion.

As soon as my mother found out she lectured me on hygiene. The farmers used their toilets on vegetables; that's where the worms came from. And then I was de-wormed. The white, frantic forms stopped falling out of me; but I expected them back.

One evening as I was sitting over myself, my sister Ilse came into the toilet to use the big mirror; she said she couldn't wait any longer. I was embarrassed but forgot about her while contemplating myself. Suddenly Ilse said: "What are you doing?! It's disgusting to look into the bowl! I'll tell mother." She went over to the chain and pulled. My soft malleable geography, my other me was slurped down the pipe against my will. I felt lonely and abandoned on the toilet, torn from the reveries with myself. The outside world had destroyed my secret self. I felt guilty and ashamed of my poor other me that was doomed to be flushed into the eternal darkness of our plumbing. I stopped looking.

◎ 9 ◎

The German Africa Corps was stopped at El Alamein. Our *Telefunken* spit out that name every night. Gertrude said that it was only temporary; we were getting our breath back before we took Egypt. We measured with a string the distance between El Alamein and Cairo. "It's nothing," Gertrude said. "We have fast tanks."

Meanwhile, in the yellow gendarmerie, I lived a happy life. Every evening after dinner my father rocked me on his knees. He had taken off his uniform jacket and sat there with his long-sleeved underwear and suspenders. We played *"Hoppe Hoppe Reiter, wenn er fällt dann schreit er."* He was the horse, I was the rider. At some point, he would open his thighs and I fell through. Though he always caught me at the last moment, I had the sensation of falling into an abyss. My stomach fluttered and soon as he caught me I begged him to start all over again. I abandoned myself to the game. I bent my head backwards and shrieked with joy. I couldn't wait for my father's knees to open. According to the rhyme that went with the game, I fell into a ditch where I was eaten by black ravens. In German, *Raben* rhymed with *graben*. Usually his thighs opened when he sang the word raven and I was swallowed up by the dark word. His head bent toward me as I fell and he laughed as he pulled me back up onto his knees. Nothing could happen to me. My father was a green gendarme in the center of the German Reich. He made the law and I was his son. My father saved me from the black ravens. He had strong thighs, he had a hairy chest; he took care of me and my mother, as well. I slept next to them in their bedroom and could hear them breathe when I woke up in the middle of the night. Their breathing sounded warm and secure and I went back to sleep.

Gendarmes were all around me. They smelled of gasoline, leather, and tobacco. Their black boots creaked. They waved at me every time they passed.

One of them lived in a small room between our apartment and the Kluges. ' His room was for unmarried gendarmes. Sometimes he came to us in the evening. When he saw me, he clicked his heels and said, *"Heil Hitler!"* Everybody laughed and I blushed.

He lifted me up to the apples where I could select one. I hesitated as I looked for the best one. In the winter, the apples were shriveled but still juicy. They made a leathery sound when I bit into them: small round explosions, white juicy meat.

Sometimes the gendarme had taken off his uniform and I saw that he wore the same underwear my father wore. I could smell his body when he lifted me up to the apples. He put his hands under my shoulders and pushed me upwards saying, *"Hoppla!"* As soon as his arms went up, the smell of his armpits rose with me simultaneously. It mingled with the fragrance of the apples. The two smells fused, and I couldn't make out any more what smelled like what. I held in my breath. I smelled my ancestors. I liked the smell; I had my ancestors' nostrils. Sometimes I bit into an apple while the gendarme still held me up. The apple was as hairy as his armpits, and I ingested both.

•   •   •

Sergeant Ritter had moved into our old apartment. Frau Ritter, who was called Frau Sergeant Ritter, also wore her hair in a bun. She shook her head in amazement and said to my mother, "You sure got a serious little boy...I've never seen such a serious little boy." She looked at me and then at my mother again. "He's too serious for his age! I can't get over it. The way he stands there all the time with his hands behind his back and looks at things gives me goose bumps...I wonder what he's thinking all the time." She looked at me but I couldn't give her an answer. I only looked. My eyes clicked away like my father's Agfa but without the clicks that announced the capture of an image. And my film was in color.

My mother was on her knees. It was her turn to wax the staircase. She was talking to Frau Lieutenant Kluge; the two women didn't see me come in the entrance hall where Hitler and Göring demanded a perfectly polished gendarmerie. I heard my mother say, "Did you hear him scream yesterday?" After a short pause, Frau Kluge's "Yes" floated down the hallways like a leaf that had just left the tree, unsure and fluttery. My mother's voice was more involved that Frau Kluge's; she seemed reserved, my mother emotional. My mother said, "Why do they have to beat them that hard...?" When I asked her about it, my mother said nobody was beaten.

But I knew the office was the only place where they could beat someone, and I began to look at the closed door with new eyes every time I passed it. I listened for screams, but heard none. I thought of our Spanish reed, a supple strong cane that my parents had bought as soon as my oldest sister was born; it was used for serious punishments only, but the threat of it was often in the air. My father only caned me once — when I refused to eat a chocolate pudding for dessert. He locked me in our bathroom first and when I still refused to eat he put me over his knees and caned me. He sat on the toilet seat while I stared at the floor. I heard the swish of the cane and then I felt a bright stinging pain on my buttocks. Since it was the only time, it stuck in my mind like a coin stuck in a vending machine.

I wondered if our Spanish reed was used for the beatings in the office. I checked for our cane; it was still in its place in the pantry. My ears were listening in the direction of the office.

•   •   •

The oleanders in the Beyers' pots were blooming. The typewriters were chattering in the office, and I helped Mr. Beyer to water his flowers. The apple gendarme was laughing above us, and I could hear the voice of my father and others. Franconian clouds sailed by in the summer blue.

Herr Beyer's watering can was made out of gray zinc; it was huge and shaped like Herr Beyer's stomach: round and vaulted. I had my own small watering can made out of white enamel. The water lapped against the bucket as I came back from the faucet. We watered next to each other. The water sounded like rain when it his the big round, veined leaves of the nasturtiums. The glossy surface repelled the water; it ran off in small clear balls, like quicksilver. Herr Beyer swung the can up and down, creating swells and lulls in the stream of the water. I searched out snails and threw them into Herr Beyer's water bucket. Otherwise they would devour the garden. Everything had its purpose and place in our garden, and I felt content in the blue summer air. The apple gendarme screamed, "You goddamned son-of-a-bitch" in the office. His voice was distorted and full with rage.

Mr. Beyer and I listened in the direction of the open office-window. Someone whimpered, then screamed and I heard the noise of shuffling chairs. A man yelled *"Nein!"* and then thuds, like the sound of my mother's rug beater when she hit the rug, only softer and muffled, came from the window. A man screamed again. I had never heard adults scream like that. It was shocking and embarrassing, because it was uncontrolled. The sounds were not connected with something I could see, but as part of some momentous drama. And while it went on, sparrows twittered in Herr Beyer's garden, snails drowned slowly in the bucket, the nasturtiums were dripping with water, and Frau Beyer had hung up laundry to dry in the sun. Screams from the office passed like a cold breeze over Frau Beyer's sheets.

Nothing happened. Herr Beyer laughed and said there they go again, beating someone's ass because he didn't tell the truth. We went back to the nasturtiums that whipped up and down like small umbrellas under the bursts from the watering cans.

◈10◈

I entered a new phase that summer. Lieutenant Röhmer, who had moved into Nüsslein's apartment, had two children. One was Wolfram, a teenager in the *Hitler Jugend*, and the other was Irmtraud, my age.

Irmtraud was born in July 1937 in a hospital in Würzburg. Her doctor had never given birth to blood sausages. He cut her navel, but it wasn't a navel from Frau Schütz. I compared hers to mine: all right, but nothing spectacular. It stuck out a little too far and was wrinkled at the end like a tiny shriveled plum. She always picked lint out of it.

Frau Lieutenant Röhmer had dark-blonde hair pulled back in a bun. She waxed her floors twice weekly and everyone except officers had to take their shoes off as soon as they stepped across the threshold. Like everyone else in the neighborhood, Frau Lieutenant Röhmer shook out her mop from her windows every morning, and beat her rugs on Fridays in the garden. They had a piano (we didn't), and Irmtraud had to play it. She was more *bürgerlich* than me.

Everybody said that Irmtraud and I were made for each other. We were a cute couple. We were the same height, the same age, had almost the same hair color-though hers was blonder than mine. We played together all the time. I invited Irmtraud into my tree house, the old wardrobe suspended in our pear tree with the tough wormy pears.

Irmtraud introduced me to dolls. Her neatly made bed was full of dolls of all sizes. Some closed and opened their eyes, some said "Mama," others were stiff and lifeless. The minute I saw them I wanted to play with them. I was willing to leave my wind-up cars behind and put bottles into the dolls' mouths and change their diapers. There was no doubt in my mind that was what I wanted to do. But everybody said dolls weren't for boys, and so I reluctantly left them on Irmtraud's bed.

The whole neighborhood pointed at us and said we were the cutest things in Kitzingen. There is a whole series of snapshots from my Irmtraud years that show us before every possible backdrop. While Hitler played Barbarossa in Russia, we played cute in front of the neighborhood Agfas — next to the lilac bushes, in front of pansies, in our garden, in the Beyers' garden, out on the street; Irmtraud with white ribbons in her hair, we both in Sunday clothes; overexposed, underexposed, out of focus, with legs, without legs, uncentered, smiling and sullen — we survive into eternity. Two Aryan kids were growing up in an abandoned monastery, surrounded by the smell of wax and polish. We have fat and happy faces.

•   •   •

Some images are forever. Against the foliage of the pear tree and the dark greens of Herr Beyer's crab grass, stand Irmtraud and her pigtails, Herr Lieutenant Röhmer's little daughter.

With Irmtraud in the gendarmerie, my life became perfect. The circumference of the old monastery was all we needed. We became Adam and Eve. Our garden became Paradise. Adults told us we were going to marry each other as soon as we grew up. They patted my head and pulled her pigtails. Wasn't that a fine idea, they asked. We smiled and looked stupid. They told me I would become a gendarme, like my father; Irmtraud would be a gendarme's wife, just like her mother; and we would have little gendarmes — little green gendarmes for the Führer; and they pointed to the pictures in the hall.

The adults coordinated my life with hers, hers with mine. They saw us as two equal parts, miniature reflections of themselves. Irmtraud believed the adults more than I did. In many of the snapshots she looks into the camera with the look of her mother on her face: she is a gendarme's wife. She looks straight into the camera, self-assured. Irmtraud knows who and what she is. I, on the other hand, often have a preoccupied smile on my face; I tend to look past the eye of the camera, into some unseen space. Whenever the adults told us to link arms, or put our arms around each other's neck's, it was Irmtraud who developed a real grip. Mine looks arranged.

My mind stored images in the sun. Easter, for example, we were the center of the universe with the air sunny, warm, and blue. The Franconian sun that day will never sink beyond the horizon. Dew was still on the grass in the Beyers' garden. The adults had pulled all strings on the black market to make us happy. They had hidden our Easter nests in the garden. I had to look first. They had padded the real grass with artificial grass; in the middle of the nest sat a big Easter rabbit made of baked dough. A red egg was coming out of his rear end. There was candy and a *papier-maché* egg. In it was a toy tank that shot sparks after it was wound up. Irmtraud found hers. She had the same rabbit, but his egg was blue. And next to it stood a toy-cooking stove. On it were frying pans with tiny pieces of meat sizzling like real meat because of candles inside the stove. Smoke curled up from the stove into the Easter air. I wanted to help cook, but I had to play with the tank.

My life was perfect. Security surrounded me; my parents thought of nothing else than to make me happy. Irmtraud shared the gendarmerie with me; Hitler and Göring were in their place; everything was in order. The Easter sun was warm, and the Beyers' grasses smelled fresh and cool and clean.

• • •

There were some irregularities in the blues and green of our garden, but Irmtraud and I absorbed them and forgot them. Irmtraud and I were in our tree house between heaven and earth, puffy clouds coasting by overhead. We were having lunch. Irmtraud had fixed salad leaves, which she served, on her little dishes. While she cleaned the kitchen, I pretended I was a gendarme sitting at his desk waiting for the phone to ring. Or, it was teatime. We drank artificial lemonade and pretended it was tea. We had black war cookies with it. And while having tea one day, it happened again. A man screamed in the office above us. The windows were open, blue smoke was curling above us as usual. We heard muddled thuds. Irmtraud said, "He's getting his ass beaten." The word "*Arsch*" sounded improper in her mouth. It shocked me. She said that her daddy had told her it happened sometimes. Then Irmtraud shouted in the direction of her mother's living room that someone was being beaten in the office. My father appeared at the office window and looked down on us. The screaming stopped, and he closed the window.

My father had looked through us. It wasn't my real father. His eyes didn't focus on us. He had the same unfocused look on his face one day when we were playing with a red and white dotted ball in the entrance hall under Hitler and Göring. The black DKW pulled up outside and my father, another gendarme, and a prisoner in handcuffs got out; they came in and passed us on the way to the office. We stopped and stared. Irmtraud had her arms behind her back and looked at the procession. I stood back and watched. My father passed without seeing us.

• • •

On gray days when Frau Röhmer wasn't there, Irmtraud and I took off our shoes and went sliding across Röhmer's polished hallway. The wax our mothers used came in round yellow cans. It smelled almost like something to eat. If I put my nose close to the brown wax, it had a full creamy texture. But it had a sting, which went right back to my throat. My mother said that this was the turpentine in it. And turpentine wasn't edible. My mother above, Frau Röhmer below, were on their knees every Friday morning and waxed the floors. As the day went on and they ran out of wax, they melted down old candles and mixed them in petroleum.

We took a running start on Frau Fohmer's floors and slid across the polish. We crossed all of the German Reich. We acted out the latest news. We placed Munich at one end of the corridor and Berlin at the other. We squeezed Warsaw to the right, next to the wardrobe. We opened the door to the living room and saw Paris spread out before us. We were express trains linking all the cities of Europe with lightning speed. The grain of the old parquet floor transmitted a hard tickling sensation through the socks to our feet. We went so fast we got dizzy. The smell of wax intoxicated us as we pushed the borders of the German Reich farther and farther until Munich was situated in the middle of the hall and Athens was in its place on the southern frontier. We screamed, we competed. Irmtraud wanted to go as far as Moscow, but I told her we didn't have it yet. Then Frau Röhmer came and threw us out because we were ruining her floors. She took out her polisher and went over them once more.

My sister Gertrude told me that Göring, our *Reichsfeldmarschall*, had said that not a single plane would penetrate the territories of the German Reich. It was an accident that they had reached Berlin. We looked at her school atlas; Germany spread into all directions. It covered blue, dark brown, light brown, and green areas. Red and black dots were cities. Kitzingen was a small black dot comfortably stuck in a bend that the Main River made between Würzberg and Nürnberg. Every time I looked at her atlas, my stomach began to flutter: I could see all of Germany in one glance. My eyes nervously traveled between Hamburg and the Alps in one second. I imagined that I was on a train following the dark railway lines criss-crossing Europe. I went to Paris, a representative of the Reich. I wore a gray officer's uniform. I took a plane, a three-motored Junkers to Warsaw; I landed in the snows of Poland wearing black boots. And, within the blink of an eye, I had covered the distance between Warsaw and Amsterdam, which I had seen in a newsreel at the movies. Our *Telefunken* announced my arrivals and departures.

We looked at Berlin. Gertrude explained that Berlin was too close to England. As for us, we were far away from Berlin; the enemy could never reach us. But, in the meantime, to be on the safe side, we had to get prepared.

Irmtraud and I gazed with big eyes at the sudden activity around the Landwehrplatz. Every cellar was inspected, including ours, to determine which ones could be used for air-raid shelters. The Beyers had a deep cellar that was declared a public shelter. Huge white letters, LSR, air-raid shelter, were painted on the yellow walls of the Benedictines. Frau Beyer cleaned out her cellar and put in boxes of sand, a fire extinguisher, and old crates and chairs along the walls for people to sit on. Anybody could use the shelter in an emergency.

Our cellar, on the other hand, was on ground level. It had gothic vaults and one window in our section at the far end. The cellar was divided into wooden partitions where the house stored wood, coal, vats of pickles and sauerkraut. We also had a pile of sand in which my mother stuck carrots to keep them fresh, next to a barrel of vinegar and a barrel of eggs in brine. Irmtraud and I never went into the cellar, because it was so dark. I came down with my mother to get sauerkraut on Fridays. We had a flashlight because there was no electricity. My mother took long prongs to pull out the sauerkraut. The lid was covered with a heavy stone. In the small circle of light I could see bayberries in the sauerkraut. When my mother lifted the lid, it made a sucking noise that echoed back from the dark. A strong pungent smell of fermenting sauerkraut arose.

Soon our cellar was full of lamps. Workmen put up iron beams to shore up the vaults in our part, because it was the safest. Our sauerkraut and barrels were moved to another partition. A little arched shelter was put up over the window to help us escape in case the main entrance should be blocked. We, too, got a box of sand — for smothering flames — and a fire extinguisher. Then our cellar was whitewashed. It was ready for us though all the adults said they would never go there during an air raid, because — in spite of the improvements — it still was above the ground and we would be pulverized immediately. We got no letters painted on our walls, because our cellar didn't qualify for a public shelter. It was only for gendarmes.

One evening we all got gas masks. Tables had been set up on the Linden Square. We lined up for the masks just before evening. Frau Lieutenant Kluge and Harald were in front of us. Harald got a tiny mask. He had to try it on, and he screamed. His voice was stifled by the green rubber. I was afraid I would suffocate when they pulled the mask over my face and was surprised that I could breathe. The masks smelled like rubber, and the air that came through the big round metal disk over the nose was sour — it reminded me of vinegar. My skin became damp under the green rubber; I panicked and pulled off the mask.

In the dusk, the people looked like giant grasshoppers. All over the Linden Square people tried on gas masks, turning around, emitting stifled sounds of surprise, showing themselves off. When my mother put on her mask and turned toward me with a lowered head, I was terrified. She was an unknown alien creature with a head much too big for her proportions. She seemed to wobble; the big filter was too heavy for her head and it pulled it downward. I stepped back in panic. My mother was a skull with two grotesque glass disks for eyes. I could hear her breathing: air was sucked in and expelled sounded threatening in the evening light. I walked backwards, away from my mother. She pulled off her gas mask and laughed.

Our gas masks came in green metal canisters. We hung them, according to instructions, in a handy place (our wardrobe in the hall) so we could grab them quickly on the way to the shelter. Sometimes Irmtraud and I took out our gas masks and put them on. We scared ourselves. We were no longer us. The masks transformed us into something horrible. We reminded ourselves dimly of what the masks stood for: terrible fire from the skies. We had heard lurid stories but didn't know the reality of them. We could only imagine them. The masks protected us from gas and smoke, but they could melt into the skin, people said, and we wouldn't be able to pull them off. The masks would become us and we would die with them. The masks were part of another self we had somewhere within it, and it appeared while we chased each other around the entrance hall under the images of Hitler and Göring. It was too scary, and we stuffed the gas masks back into their green containers.

•   •   •

The Landwehrplatz got instructions on air raids. We had drills. The sirens went off: three calm long wails meant pre-warning; a long series of fast hysterical blasts indicated immediate danger, we all had to go to the shelters. One long sustained wail told us it was all clear, we could come back out. Everybody had to check their blackout curtains.

Irmtraud and I sat in the pear tree and discussed shelters, sirens, and gas masks. Irmtraud knew more than I. She said the most dangerous part of a shelter was in the middle. The roof caved in there. We should always sit along the side. Concrete bunkers were the best, she said. And after my father took me and Irmtraud to an exhibit of enemy bombs, we discussed lengths and widths of bombs, compared ours to theirs; and we speculated on their effects.

We talked bombs for some time until Mr. Beyer gave us another topic. One day they brought a black-feathered chicken over to our side of the garden to chop off its head. The entire house stood around the clucking hen. Mr. Beyer stretched its neck over our wooden chopping block and lopped off the head with our axe. Irmtraud and I stood close to the pear tree. The headless body fell back to the ground and ran with outstretched wings in a circle before it collapsed — soundless and terrifying. Everybody pointed at the headless animal, and Irmtraud and I retreated when the hen came toward us. Her father explained it was a matter of reflexes. I didn't understand. A headless chicken had rushed towards me. It made the same motions an ordinary chicken made except it didn't have a head. I had the impression the chicken wanted to revenge itself on us. The head was lying on the bloody block. The bluish eyelids were halfway drawn over the eyes, already dead, but the body was still walking in circles. We mulled over the beheaded chicken in our tree house. I looked down on the wooden block where the hen had died. It was in its usual place and everything looked ordinary. Frau Beyer had cooked the chicken, but it didn't die in my imagination. Its headless body kept making its way toward me.

🐚12🐚

This bright morning had begun as any other. Every morning I watch the ritual of my father putting on his gun belt. To a devotional son of five years, it is the final step to his perfection that begins with his shaving at the sink. I love and worship my father at this moment. He towers over me like a mountain: mystic green, shaped by black lines. He picks up his belt by taking hold of the holster with the gun inside. I can see that it is heavy, the center of the belt's gravity; the belt is the extension of the gun; it serves to anchor my father to the gun. As he picks up the holster, the belt unfolds and lunges into shape. I anticipate its rough electric crackle, the whipping motion like a surge of energy from my father; a spark leaps to my small spine. My eyes lick my father with admiration. He sucks in air to make his waist thinner before he puts the belt around it; he must inhale before he accomplishes the final act and inhaling is an act of discipline before the belt consents to be part of him. And at this moment, I cannot distinguish my father from the holster, nor the gun inside it; his body becomes as one with the holster: *Pistolentasche*...four explosive syllables, the last part of the word the enigmatic hidden space for the gun itself. My father becomes the sound the moment he put on the belt.

I am waiting for the moment I await each morning: I watch my father's hand force the two clasps into each other. The swastika on top of the buckle slides from left to right. I listen to metal slide against metal, then comes the final click of accomplished coupling: the belt is hooked and the circuit interlocked; the sculpted swastika and the eagle slide into place, and the energy into my father: he is complete, he is powerful, he is male!

Every morning I looked forward to gorging myself on the charged perfection of my father. I believed I witnessed his soul awaken beneath the green uniform as soon as the buckle snapped into place. The symbol of the law gave his body shape; it lodged against his waist, pushing his chest outward, upward. The male existed only within a uniform, the natural male pigment; it encompassed his nature, and his nature was a coiled spring electrified and released by the frosty metallic click of the locking gun belt.

•   •   •

A beautiful spring morning in 1942, sunny and brilliant. It is in the nature of things that the Jews should leave on the noon train. It has happened that my father, the gendarme, will be in charge of the entire operation. Over a cup of barley coffee at the kitchen table, he says to my mother: "It's not fair to ask us to do it! It's not our responsibility!" My mother nods her head in silent agreement.

When I come downstairs, the *Judenschule* is surrounded by the police. The red building seems alive, full of unseen creatures. Sometimes a shadow appears at a window, but is quickly drawn back inside.

I ask my mother about this. She is at the stove. She turns down the flame and without looking once at me says carefully, "Oh, they are Jewish people, they were moved in during the night — they're not staying long, there're leaving on the noon train."

My mother then says, "go play in the garden today, your farther doesn't want you out in the street."

But I don't listen; I go stand at the corner of our house in the shade, so my father — my beloved gun-belted, uniformed hero — cannot see me.

My father, the other gendarmes and the city police are milling around in front of the school. Over them, a tall, thin, white-haired old man wearing a pince-nez stands at one of the upper windows. He shakes his fist at the street below, then suddenly two arms pull him back. But the old man reappears: he pops up again like a puppet in a punch-and-Judy show, jerky and violent. The old man shouts: "I refuse…you scum." He uses the word *Abschaum*, an old-fashioned and solemn word. Then again, two ghostly arms pull him back inside.

Below, the gendarmes and police are chattering with each

other, laughing as always. It seems like a holiday, a *Kermesse*, animated, full of life. It is the old man in the window who is out of place in the ordinariness of life on the Landwehrstrasse.

But my father is acting strange. His behavior keeps me well back in the shadows. He makes me feel guilty, watching him. He stands motionless in his green uniform in front of the open doors of the *Judenschule* and stares at the pavement with such intensity that I expect him to receive a message at any moment from the silent ground.

Again, the old man appears at the window. His behavior, too, is strange and embarrassing to me. When he shouts the same words again — You scum! — one of the gendarmes pulls out his gun and, laughing, points it at the window. My father looks up, and then orders the officer to put the gun away.

Another fist emerges from one of the upstairs windows of the *Judenschule*. It is a brown, old woman's fist, attached to a skinny arm. The fist quivers in the morning light, then is shaken up and down at the police below. No sound accompanies the motion and nobody seems to notice the gesture that takes place above the heads of the gendarmes. The solitary protest is swallowed up by noise and excitement is in the street. The fist seems to want to strike my father on the head. But he has turned his back on it, and has seen nothing. I stare at the fist from my corner, half-hidden, I don't dare step openly into the street.

Clothes are hanging in the fir trees in front of the red school. My eyes are caught by a white slip, silky and shimmering as the breeze lifts it back and forth. It dangles by its shoulder strap.

The white, silk slip seems shameless and indiscreet: my mother keeps her undergarments neatly folded in dark drawers. But no one seems offended. In fact, nobody notices. No one is at the windows along the Linden Square. Across the street, Frau Baumann's bedding is hung out as usual, but she is nowhere to be seen. Nobody passes along the street except the gendarmes and police, who mill festively in front of the school. The police ignore the shocking undergarment; and they ignore a pair of long johns swinging from the top of the farthest tree.

Suddenly from one of the upper windows of the Jewish school a large case flies out and into the street. It breaks open and silver forks and spoons scatter over the Landwehrstrasse. The gendarmes duck. A china coffeepot follows. It lands not far from me against the yellow walls of our gendarmerie. The pot has a flowery pattern. It bursts into hundreds of pieces against the wall but the spout stays intact and rolls toward me. It is graceful, shaped like a slender torso, shiny, new, with traces of the flower pattern, ready to pour coffee at any moment. I retreat from the shiny object and hide in the shadows. One of the policemen bends and gathers up the silver spoons and forks and puts them back into the case. He even breathes against the silver and polishes it on his sleeves, taking a long time doing it, then carefully tucks the case on the ledge of one of the lower windows of the Beyer house.

Somebody is emptying a briefcase of paper into the street from the upper floor of the *Judenschule*; little pieces fall in excited patterns and scatter over the juniper bushes. A voice shouts down from the same window, "You won't get anything from me! I'd rather destroy it than let you get your dirty paws on it!"

Other hands throw out more shredded papers. My father has his back to the building and doesn't notice this snowstorm. As I watch, little white balls fragment into tiny pieces that float silently to the ground. Boxes now begin to sail out of the windows…and as if that were the cue, a policeman plunges inside; I can hear him shout, OUT! EVERYBODY OUT!

One of the gendarmes is striking the iron grills on the ground floor windows with his nightstick. It makes a deep echo inside the school. The sound is effective. Invisible creatures from the inside are streaming out as if the sound of the nightstick is too much for their ears. Men, women, children: the old man with the pince-nez is there too; he's on the arm of a young girl, muttering to himself. Everybody is carrying a small suitcase, even the children. A thin old woman appears. She has a long, skinny nose like the beak of a bird; her glasses have slid far down. She is wearing a brown coat and a brown hat with flowers on it. She steps right up to my father and shouts: "You can't do this!" *"Ich gehe nicht! Hören Sie? Ich gehe nicht!"* She pushes her face right into my father's. He looks straight past her, he says nothing. The apple gendarme takes hold of the old woman's arm and leads her back into the column of people.

My father walks to the head of the column and stands with his back to the group. He knows the other gendarmes are taking their positions without orders from him. He looks straight through the big opening for the overpass of the Neue Brücke, as if perceiving a mysterious vision at the beginning of the Glauberstrasse, a vision markedly different from the event that is occurring behind his back. He begins to walk and the column follows; he doesn't even turn to see if the group is in motion; he seems to know that they will follow. I think: where he goes, they go. From shadows my eyes pursue this double man: green uniform, black boots, black belt with a gun holster. His eyes are hooked into an invisible groove before him; a track pulls him ahead. He is following a voice I cannot hear; I'm drawn to follow him, like the Jews. We walk up the hill, turn left, walk under the hawthorn trees in bloom: white, pink, red. My father grasps the holster with his right hand. It gives him a rigidly forked shape; he is strong, he is authority. He is The Law.

The column marches up the Würzburger Strasse until it reaches the Falterturm, where it turns left. I am following, hidden in the shadows of the bushes along the avenue. We leave the gas works behind and turn into the Adolf Hitler Strasse, which leads to the train station. Suddenly, the thin old woman steps out of the column and begins to shout. She shakes her fist at the gendarmes, then at my father, who doesn't see her. The apple gendarme laughs, grabs her arm, pats her on the back: *"Du alte Giftnudel, du…"* "You poisonous old noodle, can't you be quiet?" But the woman stubbornly sets her suitcase on the ground. Her voice is high and shrill, it rises above all the noise on the street. The column begins to fall apart. The old woman has her arms high in the air and is waving them back and forth; her mouth forms shrieking words I do not understand. Near her is a little boy about my age carrying a small suitcase. He is wearing long brown stockings under his short pants; I am wearing the same. One of the gendarmes penetrates the column and gives the old woman a gentle shove; he says, "Will you get on now, you crazy old woman?" The column slowly begins to move again beneath the towering chestnut trees. In the gardens in front of the old houses along the Adolf Hitler Strasse the hawthorn trees are in bloom, exploding with color.

At the end of the wide avenue I can see the station. I stop and watch from behind the grill of the freight yard. A train stands belching black smoke on platform three, its old third-class carriages with no connecting platforms, the kind of train we take to Würzburg. The gendarmes motion the people from the *Judenschule* to various carriages. The owlish old woman is pushed into a carriage: but she won't climb the steps. One of the gendarmes pushes against her back, but the old woman braces herself against the steps and the hand rail, dropping her umbrella. The gendarme picks it up and pushes her again…someone inside the train grabs her hands, and pulls her in. The gendarme waves, laughs, and slams the door. The old woman emerges, her hat crooked. She stands again on the steps, shaking the umbrella at the gendarme. He points at her and shouts *"Die spinnt doch!"* "She's nuts!" The old woman cries, *"Verbrecher!"* "Gangsters! I won't leave!" In mock exasperation, the gendarme lifts his shoulders for his comrades. He yells back at her: "You'll go back inside now and go off, if it's the last thing I'll do…!" And he grabs her again and heaves her up into the carriage, laughing all the time… *"Du verrückte Alte, will'st jetzt ruhig sein?"* "You crazy old woman, shut up!" The gendarme slams the door and motions to my father, as if inviting him to laugh, but my father is staring blankly in the direction of Würzburg, to the west, where we always visit my mother's friend who has an orchard in the hills. The train begins to move — direction Nürnberg. The old woman leans out of the window; she shakes her umbrella at the gendarmes on the platform. The ancient locomotive gathers speed. I run home as fast as I can.

My father never knows that I watched him that bright morning.

When I returned home, the Jewish school looked as if it had never been inhabited. The clothes were gone from the trees and bushes; all the papers had been picked up. The owl lady and the old man with the pince-nez could have an invention of my childish mind. I overtook Frau Lachmann and another woman, who were carrying a rolled-up rug. The rug was too heavy for them, and the women walked with bent knees at a fast clip, as if they couldn't wait to get home. Their faces were covered with sweat as they stopped for a moment to breathe. Frau Lachmann shouted that I should tell my mother that genuine Persian rugs were being auctioned off for next to nothing at the Hotel Bavarian Court. She shouted, tell her to hurry, the best things are already gone!

But my mother knew already about the Persian rugs. Frau Beyer was there, talking to her. Frau Beyer had bought three of them "cheap as dirt." She said over and over again in a firm voice that they had been bought "legally, very legally, everything was in the open!" — that the government itself had sold them, "therefore, there was nothing to worry about." My mother was unusually quiet, but Frau Beyer hadn't noticed. Frau Beyer opened a big bundle and pulled out two fur coats. "Persian lamb...who would have thought I would own one of these...!" The other coat was Russian sable. Frau Beyer took my mother's hand and made her feel the fur. While she caressed the furs, Frau Beyer's voice climbed to an unnatural pitch. I could hear the saliva collecting in her mouth; her voice slurred. "Pre-war work," she said. "Look at it! What quality! The lining is silky, like a baby's behind!"

That same afternoon my mother shared a cup of linden tea with Frau Kluge in our kitchen. I sat on the bench and watched them. My mother said she wanted no part of this; she couldn't live in a house that had "unjust things." Frau Kluge laughed and said that the best coats and rugs of the "Jewish loot" had already been shipped to Würzburg for the wives of high officials. Frau Beyer hadn't gotten such a bargain, she said; the coats had some bare spots. Frau Kluge asked, "Can you imagine Frau Beyer walking across her oriental rugs in her Russian sable coat?" She laughed; she called Frau Beyer a dirty peasant one day and the owner of Persian rugs and fur coats the next. "It will be interesting to watch the neighbors during winter," said Frau Kluge, "to see how many of them suddenly turn up in fur coats."

As I sat there, I imagined legions of neighbors running through the streets in thick fur coats. Only my mother would be wearing the old black cloth coat she had bought from Pfarrweisach. I felt sorry for her. I couldn't understand why she didn't take one of those fabulous coats. Nobody explained anything to me; my eyes and ears gathered suggestions from the air. The rugs, the silver, the furs had a dark origin. Nevertheless, they made everybody happy! The objects had fallen "out of the blue," a fantasy come true. They made Frau Beyer stutter and perspire with excitement, yet on the streets one didn't talk about them. And when, in the cold of winter, a neighbor would appear in an unfamiliar mink coat, people would nudge each other and wink but say nothing. She could have been born in that coat! It had always been on her body.

Only Frau Beyer would break the code of silence and exclaim, "Oh, it's beastly cold this year! You're doing right, you know…wearing your fur coat!"

• • •

Not long after the Jews had departed in the direction of Nürnberg, my mother took me along to visit a friend whose husband was in the administration in Würzburg. When we entered their apartment, my mother stopped as if she had been blinded. The floor was ablaze with oriental rugs. But they were not mentioned. The lady served us from an unfamiliar coffee set. My mother acted as if she had always been served from it. The woman breathed on the silver and wiped away spots with a soft cloth, carefully replacing each piece on the ornate tray. Her eyes glowed.

Back in Kitzingen, I heard my mother say to Frau Kluge that the middle-class friends in Würzburg suddenly owned a luxury apartment. Overnight! She shook herself, as if she had goose pimples and said she couldn't live with "other people's things."

All around me in other homes that winter there were ghosts: they had slipped in with certain objects that made the apartments shine. These objects had a suspect character to them — my mother said so. I was afraid to touch them. The objects belonged to mysterious "others." They radiated something I could not understand.

•　•　•

My father refused to make an appearance in the muted discussions concerning the fabulous new objects. He shakes his head vaguely when someone mentions them, but mainly he remains stern and silent.

Later, when we discover he has kept a secret diary, we find that my father wrote carefully, with a sharp, thin pencil. His letters are tiny and strong in outline, like the lines in an engraving. Immediately after my birth in 1937, my father makes his first entry. He does not make another entry until the Jews are removed from the school that bright and sunny day and marched in the long column to the train station. He leaves two blank pages between my birth and the Jewish march, as if he wanted a cushion between the two events. On the page opposite this entry is a painting: Hitler marching toward the Feldherrnhalle in Munich during his Putsch in the twenties. Hitler is raising his right hand in a heroic gesture to the guns of the opposition. Across from Hitler my father writes:

May 1942. *The lieutenant managed to be out of town. Convenient for him. It's embarrassing. Must stay above the whole sordid mess. Finish it as quickly as possible.*

When he closed the calendar, the portrait of Hitler spread itself all over the entry.

§13§

D espite appearances, our isn't-it-too-cute-for-words Agfa-marriage wasn't a total commitment for either one of us. Irmtraud and I had our private lives. For one thing, Irmtraud had started the piano. She had to practice scales on a shiny, black upright in the half-darkened living room that was used only for holidays. Her mother offered the use of their piano to me. Both she and my mother would tell me to listen to Irmtraud as she did her scales, and then they asked me if I would like to do the same. I wasn't interested. The solemn, waxed and polished room gave me goose bumps. It was chilly there even in the summer. A photograph of Hitler hung on the wall facing the piano. Frau Röhmer had put a branch of oak leaves over the top of the photograph; the leaves were dark brown. They were as senseless as the room. Irmtraud's scales were as artificial as the red paper roses on top of the piano. Whenever she finished, Irmtraud had to take a woolen rag and wipe off fingerprints from the shiny piano. It looked like her mother wanted the lingering scales removed from the immaculate room. The scales were a temporary derangement of the room's permanent order. The piano stool had to be put back in exactly the same position that it occupied before Irmtraud started. The scales were solemn and without life. They scared me. "He doesn't have the discipline for the piano," Frau Röhmer said. My mother shook her head slowly. The black upright was a coffin that emitted unnatural sounds. They had no purpose, no connection to anything. I decided against the piano, choosing instead the blue, undisciplined air in preference to the wax-scented interiors of the Röhmer's.

Wifeless, I went for walks by myself. I could hear Irmtraud playing the upright as I left the house. Her sad, tinkering scales hobbled on broken legs through the gendarmerie and fell to the ground by the time they reached the rear wall of the garden. I wandered off into different directions, down into the technical emergency service, for example. I watched the mechanics repair dark green army trucks and ambulances. I could see the river at a distance but wasn't allowed to go that far. My mother always told me I could drown in it. So I made my way back to the square.

At the Linden Square nothing happened. Afternoons were quiet. I saw gendarmes come out of our house; people drove by on bicycles. The noise of the pedals and unoiled chains were the only sounds, except for the high-pitched mechani-

81

cal saws that came from the two carpenter shops at the north end of the square. The sound rose and fell like slow, undulating waves. I walked off into the direction of the saws.

• • •

Two carpenter shops stood on the north end of the square. One belonged to Herr Lohmann, the other to Herr Heim. I didn't like Herr Lohmann and nobody else liked him either because he quarreled with the neighbors. My mother once said that he had a lawsuit with someone over two feet of space between their houses. I didn't know what lawsuits were, but I knew that Herr Lohmann had reddish hair and a squint. I didn't like people with red hair. I didn't care if women had red hair, but I had a physical revulsion for men with red hair and pale skin. Whenever a man with red hair visited us, I had to be forced by my parents to shake hands with him. Herr Lohmann had red hair. During the summer and far into the fall, Herr Lohmann wore short pants under his long gray work coat. His naked legs were white like cheese and terminated in black socks and sandals. Crossing the square he looked like an ungainly, furless dog.

On special days Herr Lohmann wore a black uniform with short pants. His white legs looked even whiter then. In uniform, he led a column of Hitler Youths. Once, while we watched the column march by, a neighbor whispered in my mother's ear, "Look at that inflated toad! He thinks he's hot shit!" She also told her that Herr Lohmann was one of those who had set fire to the synagogue during the *Kristallnacht*. He had supplied the wood shavings from his shop to set the synagogue fire. The lady called him a fast little weasel and a firebug to boot.

From that point on, Herr Lohmann turned into a weasel with two naked human legs. I had seen a weasel once in a cage and knew what they looked like. In my imagination, I saw him running across the Landwehrplatz, his hands full of shavings, his eyes glowing red, and his legs white in the dark, his coattail flying in the wind. The fire blazed up inside the sleeping synagogue.

I always stayed away from Herr Lohmann. He was dangerous, he repelled me, yet I watched him out of the corners of my eyes when he came out of his shop. My eyes were drawn to his legs: naked, hairless, pale as unripe cheese.

Herr Heim, the other carpenter of the Landwehrplatz, was different. I remember little about him. He wore long pants, never talked, and had white hair combed straight back above his blue eyes. He nodded to me without smiling when I came into his shop.

Herr Heim's shop was low and rectangular. It was always warm there, even in winter. Whereas I knew Herr Lohmann's apprentices only from afar because they were part of their master, I knew Herr Heim's apprentices very well. They wore blue working outfits and square caps. Some wore short pants in the summer, but unlike Herr Lohmann, their legs were hairy, muscular, and tanned. I compared theirs to his when they played soccer on the Linden Square during lunch break. Herr Lohmann had two huge photographs of Himmler and Baldur von Schirach in his shop; Herr Heim didn't.

Herr Heim ran a strict shop, but he was fair (my mother had told me). Nobody talked unless addressed by Herr Heim, the Meister. Everybody had to be punctual to the minute, and the older apprentices hit the younger ones on their heads if they did something wrong. The apprentices all knew their places in the shop. At the top, right after the master, was the oldest boy, the master-apprentice. Then came the others in descending order, the youngest being the lowest and slave to all the others. He had to run and do what the others asked him. He couldn't refuse anything. He wasn't allowed to defend himself — that would have been against the shop's order. That's the way it simply was: the youngest, called a *Stift,* always had to succumb to orders. I felt sorry for him. I imagined myself in his place and was glad I still lived securely with my parents under the big roof, the Benedictine's mansard. What struck me, and scared me most in Herr Heim's shops, was the unrelenting order of things and the seemingly arbitrary actions that everybody took against the young apprentice. They called him asshole, idiot; they threatened to beat him up if he didn't work harder; and all the time they laughed. They knew what they were doing and yet they did it. He tried to please everybody, but in spite of his efforts the master apprentice kicked his rump and told him he was too slow. I wondered if he had a mother, and I felt sorry for both of them.

While Irmtraud played her lonely scales, on the black coffin, I sat in the fine white dust of Herr Heim's carpenter shop and watched the master apprentice who was just getting ready to take his master's exams. The fine dust on his face looked like snow on his eyebrows and lashes. He and the others wore the dust as gauzelike masks.

His hands were miraculous. He *was* his hands. They were big and blue-veined and had a life of their own. They moved across tables, measured things with an angular, metallic measuring iron, cut things apart, hammered them together, produced different shapes, giving different once-independent forms a new common form. His hands did it all. They were the center. Everything came from them. I wanted to lick the sawdust off them.

I sat on a chair in the corner. The room smelled of wood, sharp and dark and pleasant. Old wood had a different smell from new or wet wood. Old wood smelled like a soft warm smoke; wet wood was strong and stringent, like a wet Christmas tree.

The master apprentice never looked at me while he worked. He cut wood, his left hand holding the board, the veins on top swelling under the pressure while his right drove nails with the hammer. Sometimes he gave me part of his sandwich for lunch. I was supposed to be at home eating my mother's lunch. The first time Herr Heim offered me a part of his sandwich, I shook my head and murmured, "No, thank you." Yet I accepted the apprentice's sandwich. His hands had small cuts and abrasions. The skin of his index finger was black, with sawdust under the nail and dried glue in the lines. The glue, in a big pot on one of the tables, was golden-brown and transparent like the resin on fir trees, but it smelled sharp and slightly noxious. Its smell always rushed to the back of my head.

Having become curious about where I spent so much of my time, my mother once asked Herr Heim if I were in the way. He said, "Oh no! Winfried wants to become a carpenter when he's grown up." I looked at him in surprise. I didn't want to go out in the *Stift's* isolation and be pummeled by everyone. Watching the apprentice was all of the carpenter's world I wanted. He pulled me there, and he made me forget Irmtraud. He hypnotized me as he fed pieces of wood through the automatic saw. The veins on his hands ran down from the knuckles to the wrists. The tendon running down from his thumb was gigantic and moved the hair on the back of his hands. The hair powdered with wood dust, looked like tall grass down at the river under a thin cover of snow, or like fine white flour that covered the crust of dark bread. When the apprentice handed me a piece of his bread, I couldn't see the difference between the bread and the skin of his fingers.

Each visit to Herr Heim's shop precipitated the next. During my solitary afternoons, I was pulled there like a rambling bug tied to an invisible rope held by the master apprentice. My eyes took picture after picture of the apprentice. He was drafted into the army shortly after his exams and disappeared from view, but he was stored forever in my psychic camera. Irmtraud had no idea I had been willingly apprenticed to an apprentice. While she sat entombed in her living room in front of her polished black piano, I took in with wide-open eyes the veins, skin, and bones of the shape of hands in the warm, dust-filled and resin-scented shop of Herr Heim.

•   •   •

As soon as Irmtraud and I were together I put apprentices behind me and did what was expected of me. According to our album, I eternally offered her my arm for our official Agfa portraits, those frozen little moments in German history. On Franconian Sunday afternoons, Irmtraud and I are positioned in front of a villa-like house, white, proper, white fence, neat bushes behind the fence: the suburbs of Kitzingen. Our parents wanted the proper background for us. *"Sehr gepflegt,"* my mother called that type of house. She always dreamed of *"ein Häuschen"* of her own. And there we were: I was as usual in my suit, all buttoned up, with the short pants. Irmtraud on my right arm is wearing a light-colored coat, big buttons, white collar, ribbon in her hair, with forget-me-nots. The ribbon looks like a huge ruffled butterfly perching on a mount of thin hair after long and tiring flight. She carries a sprig of blooming hawthorn in her right hand. She looks smug and sluggish to the camera; I, on the other hand, have a posed but friendly smile, my I-know-what-I'm-supposed-to-do smile. On the back of the snapshot, Gertrude wrote in green ink: "Winfried, four-and-a-half years old. 1942." Summer, Sunday clothes, Sunday Agfa: two neat Aryan kids out for a walk. Franconia is quiet; we look pleased with ourselves.

▧14▧

S ome events don't just happen. They have roots in the past, long before my ancestor Georg Adler. When they happen they expose hidden landscapes: boiling sulfur pits, and rumblings of volcanic eruptions.

On one of my wanderings away from Irmtraud I met a small cat. A brief encounter, but the cat clawed its way into my brain and memory. It happened on a sunny day in the late morning down at the river where the mist was rising from the water. I can't remember how it started except that I disobeyed one of the basic rules all the children around the Landwehrplatz were supposed to follow.

As soon as we had come to Kitzingen, I was told to stay away from the *Siedlungskinder*, the kids from the public housing project in the east of the city, along the road to Mainbernheim. The settlement housed workers, their families and welfare cases. The kids had to come into town for school each day. Every morning and afternoon they walked along the Landwehrstrasse.

The other children and I who lived along the Landwehrplatz stayed out of sight when they arrived. We watched them from behind the linden trees, at home close to our doors. The kids from the settlement, so we were told, were dirty, had no manners, and meant trouble. Whenever we did something we weren't supposed to do, our parents told us that we behaved like *Siedlungskinder* and if we didn't stop doing whatever we were doing, we would have to live in the Siedlung. It was clear to us, to live there was exile and punishment. It was a pit of rats and snakes. The people who lived there were nearly as low as gypsies. As a matter of fact, for me the Siedlung was worse than a gypsy camp because I had never seen gypsies, while I saw children from the settlement every day. Their clothes didn't fit. The pants and sleeves were too small. They didn't have gloves, and in the winter they breathed on their hands to warm them. They didn't have handkerchiefs. They blew their noses through their fingers, flung the snot far into the street, or if the snot ran down their lips, they sucked it in and swallowed it. *"Pfui Teufel!"* my mother always said, "It's disgusting. Don't you dare use your fingers like that!"

Nobody ever thought of going to the Siedlung. I had seen it only from afar on our Sunday walks to the forest: little white houses with tall red gables. It belonged to a territory nobody wanted. Even the children there seemed to know it. They walked down the Landwehrstrasse, alien territory for them, in large groups as if they wanted to protect themselves. But they didn't need protection; we did.

The boys were taller than I was, stronger, too, and aggressive. I was told they had gang wars on the fields along the river, with clubs, rocks, and big dogs. I, accustomed to the protection of the Benedictines' walls, couldn't imagine myself taking part in a war. I thought of the dogs and shuddered. I watched the boys from the Siedlung come by; I was repelled and fascinated. My eyes followed them all the way down the Linden Square.

The *Siedlungskinder* saw us living on the other side of things. They chased us down the street and called us assholes, weaklings, cowards, shits, and turds. In the winter, they threw snowballs at us, rubbed snow into our faces, saying that we needed washing, or stuffed it down our backs. To get snow down my back was next to death.

We didn't defend ourselves. We knew we were superior — our parents had told us so. We blew our noses into handkerchiefs. Sometimes, from the safety of our doors, we shouted *"Siedlungskinder"* after them. It was the deadliest insult we could come up with. The *Siedlungskinder* came and went every day. We watched them like beings from another world. Dangerous beasts. They had strong smells, the *Siedlungsmell*, the other-side-of-the-track smell, strong like wet dogs.

And one day as I was talking to a group of *Siedlungskinder* (I can't remember how it got started), the leader asked me to play *Räuber und Schander* (Cops and Robbers) with them along the river. I accepted; a truce was established. Both sides were flattered. For them I was a prize, a policeman's son. I had mingled feelings of guilt and excitement, knowing I was entering forbidden territory, ignoring my mother's taboos. I abandoned myself to the *Siedlungskinder*. Although the leader's sleeves were too short for his arms, I was ready to follow his orders. I winced nervously at his language. He called the others *Arschlöcher* and *Hosenscheisser,* assholes and shit-in-the-pants. But I was dazzled by the way he pulled it off. He was what he was and he knew it.

A small tiger-striped cat walked along the other side of the street while we were getting organized. The cat stopped, looked over at us, and trustingly meowed. The kids from the settlement asked me if I knew the cat. I said no, since I had never seen it. They said it was therefore a homeless cat, and the best and humane solution for stray cats was death. The leader picked up the purring cat, and the group followed him down to the river. He stroked the cat in his arms.

I was struck dumb by the logic of the *Siedlungskinder*. I didn't know if the cat was homeless or not. I liked cats. I had inherited that emotion from Gertrude who brought every stray cat and dog into our homes. She fed them and purred to them like a cat herself. A cat was warm, furry, and needed attention. I had always seen them through my sister's eyes as something nearly sacred. And now I was following a doomed cat down to the river. Something terrible was going to happen. I hoped the *Siedlungskinder* weren't serious. But they were. All the way down they discussed cats. They had a mission: to put stray cats out of their misery.

When I saw the river appear at the bottom of the Technische Nothilfe, my stomach fluttered with nervousness. At the same time excitement was turning over in my groin, my scrotum contracted. We walked along the cemented dock area where the ships picked up gravel and cement sacks. We went through the arch of the Neue Mainbrücke and reached the grassy wild banks of the river. Nobody came down here during the week. It was the perfect place for crime.

Our leader took the cat by its tail and flung it around his head a few times. The cat let out a mortified scream. The boy let go. The cat, with all its four legs stiffly pointing outward as if it wanted to brake the air, sailed across the sky, through the light morning mist, into the river. It hit the water with a splash, went under, surfaced, and swam quickly toward the shore, with its head high.

As the cat made its way through the faint morning mist toward the banks, I knew I was standing on unknown ground, suspended between the scene I saw before me and the Benedictines behind me. I had ventured out of our garden with an alien group and saw dangerous blackness behind the misty riverbanks. Cats were drowned in it; I watched a drowning cat. Should I join the *Siedlungskinder* and help drown the cat, whirl the cat by its tail, flay it alive, and outdo them? Or should I save the cat and risk being beaten up? I did nothing. I stepped back a few more paces and watched, crossed between horror and excitement.

We ran along the riverbank to the spot where the cat came ashore. It had lost its fluffiness and was skinny and dripping. It meowed at us as if it wanted to tell us that we had done a terrible thing but were forgiven. The cat shook itself, and the leader picked it up and threw it back into the river. The *Siedlungskinder* threw stones and rocks at the cat. The current carried it downstream. The stones made little fountains rise all around the swimming animal as it tried for shore again. As soon as it reached shore, the cat was thrown back in. Big drops of water swirled out of its fur as the cat flew through the sunny morning. I was perspiring with fear and guilt, as I followed the *Siedlungskinder* down the river.

After the fourth or fifth time, the cat showed signs of exhaustion. It could barely crawl out of the water, and it was thrown back in. The cat tried again for the shore, going under a few times, coming back up, when a big rock hit it right on the spine below the head. The cat went down with the rock and didn't surface again.

I had hoped the cat might escape somehow and I was

shocked by its sudden and ultimate disappearance. The hazy river had swallowed it forever and nothing could make it vomit up the cat again.

A short silence followed the cat's death. The leader of the group said the cat was now put out of its misery. I told him I had to go home for lunch. I ran fast across the grass. At lunch, I tasted the cat in my mouth. Nothing was the same, though the sun and the dew on the grass were as pristine as usual. The cat wouldn't go away. I didn't dare to talk about it at home. Nobody could take the cat off my mind.

A few days later, I sat with Irmtraud in the pear tree, and suddenly, while she was pouring our tea, I told her the cat story. She sat there with her mouth wide open. I expected moral outrage. Irmtraud closed her mouth and then after some reflection she asked me to tell her again how many times the cat had come to shore before it drowned. I looked at her with surprise. "Cats, you know," she said, "are tough. They have nine lives and it's hard to kill them off."

Irmtraud's reaction made her my accomplice. By not condemning me, she had joined me. I was sure she would have done the same thing in my place. I felt that she had taken off part of my guilt and placed it on herself.

§15§

Sometimes during 1942 my father decided to become an officer. While Irmtraud and I played gendarme and wife in the pear tree, my parents felt that an officer would offer greater advantages to his family. He went for officers' training to Freiburg in the Black Forest.

"Dear Little Bird," he wrote me on one of his postcards, "I'm sending you best wishes from the Black Forest. It's very beautiful here. Listen to your mother, be a good little boy. Your father." I got another card from him: a photograph of an inn in a valley of the Black Forest. It was written a day before my fifth birthday, November 9, 1942, exactly one-day after General Eisenhower had surprised the Germans by landing in north Africa. The postmark slants across the face of Adolf Hitler on the blue stamp. My father said, "Yesterday we searched all day for a Polish murderer in the mountains. We didn't find him. We stopped here at the inn after walking ten kilometers across valleys and mountains. It's so peaceful here. One day I shall bring you to the Black Forest. Your Father."

My father worked hard; he was tired and complained to my mother he was getting too old for learning things. He studied National Socialist philosophy, leadership, criminology, criminal and civic law, and had to take sports. He rose at 5:30 every morning because classes started at 6:30. They ended at nine o'clock in the evening. In a letter to my mother he wrote: "As soon as I get back home we'll celebrate with a good bottle of wine." That letter of October 3, 1942 went on: "I'm glad to hear Gertrude got an A in English. Tell her to continue like that. I'm afraid I won't be getting any As here — I'll be satisfied to get through with Cs…P. S. Last night we spent three hours in an air-raid shelter."

My mother sent big parcels with wine, cakes, cards for his name day, cigarettes for his birthday, which was four days before mine. He sent us cans of rare pork meat. He took a day off with four comrades and rode an aerial tramway up a high mountain. "It's a magnificent countryside," he wrote.

"The leaves are turning now; in the morning, light fog was covering the valleys..." He missed us, and always closed his letters with: "...my love to the children," and he often added, "especially to Winfried. Your husband and father."

For my birthday he sent me handmade toys from the Black Forest — in spite of shortages and his heavy schedule at the academy in Freiburg. From Frau Schütz I got a birthday card, saying that all was well in Pfarrweisach, except poor Herr Kuhn was still a guard in Oranienburg. All was not so well in other places though. General Eisenhower was advancing in north Africa, and in Russia we got stuck at Stalingrad. Anyway, we had a cake, drank a toast to Frau Schütz, I fondled my navel, and then we looked up north Africa and Stalingrad in Gertrude's atlas. Stalingrad was on a big blue vein called Volga; north Africa was at the sea. "Rommel will throw the Anglo-American forces right back into the sea," Gertrude told me, and I believed her.

My father finished with Cs in all his courses, three points above the class average. He got a large certificate, with eagles, swastikas, and signatures by commanders and the Führer. It was signed and stamped on December 18, 1942. In Russia things weren't going so well. The entire gendarmerie talked about Stalingrad and my father wrote that he would be home for Christmas. But before my father came back, I had to face St. Nikolaus.

•   •   •

St. Nikolaus appeared on December 6. He had a long white beard and came from cold forests in the north. He carried a big bag with apples and candy for good children, and had a helper who punished the bad ones, called Knecht

Rupprecht. He carried an empty bag with a chain tied around his middle. St. Nikolaus had records of children's behavior in a black ledger. He knew everything.

In December 1942, I had reasons to be afraid of St. Nikolaus. There was a black entry under my name in his ledger — everybody told me so. They said there was no telling what would happen to me on December 6. Fear was taking hold of me because a few weeks earlier I had picked up a high-pressure hose which a gendarme used for washing the black DKW and I turned it into Frau Ritter's open bedroom window. I made circles with the jet of water and funneled it through the window. The water splashed and gurgled as it hit the walls and the feather beds. Frau Ritter's eiderdown pillows and covers filled with the feathers of generations of Franconian chickens (handed down as heirlooms) soaked up water like gigantic sponges. I dropped the hose after I heard a crash inside as the Ritters' big portrait of a madonna over their beds fell to the floor. As I ran toward the Linden Square I heard a terrible scream come from Frau Ritter's bedroom.

For several days the flood in Ritters' bedroom outdid the news coming form Russia. My mother had to pay for all damages and the story spread around the Linden Square. Frau Ritter said she would come upstairs to see my punishment by St. Nikolaus.

Knecht Rupprecht's long chain dragged over the cobblestones that led up to our door. Knocks and hollow sounds came up from the darkness. A bell rang. Nikolaus and Rupprecht went to Irmtraud first. I stood at our door and listened. Irmtraud let our terrified shriek. I slammed the door.

There was no escape; I had to face the black ledger. My

ears pounded, my eyes throbbed, my mind was reeling. I dimly saw Irmtraud with a streaked face, still sobbing, standing in the doorway next to Frau Ritter who nodded and said, "Rupprecht is going to get you!"

St. Nikolaus asked me if I flooded Frau Ritter's bedroom. My mouth went dry, nothing came out. I faced myself in the black book in St. Nikolaus' hands, and all I could do was nod. My face was hot, my ears burned. The gendarme whose hose I had used for spraying the bedroom came to testify. He said I was the only one around the DKW that day. He pointed at me, Frau Ritter wagged her index finger at me, and I looked at my mother who stood in the shadow. I felt alone on an empty plain.

St. Nikolaus pronounced sentence: several months with Knecht Rupprecht. He shook his chains and came with the open sack toward me. I wanted to run, but the gendarme held me and Rupprecht pulled the sack over my head. It smelled like potatoes. I was going to be put away like a potato. I let out a blood-curdling scream.

My mother saved me. She came from across the corridor and told Knecht Rupprecht that I had learned my lesson. But, she said, if I wasn't going to be a good boy during the coming year, he could take me a year from now.

16

M y heart slowly calmed as I heard Rupprecht's rattling chain recede in the distance. He returned to the forests of the north, they said. But he would be back…I had one year to recover. A year was a long time; so long that I couldn't even imagine it. I was safe. An endless shaft of time protected me until the next coming of St. Nikolaus. And in the meantime my father came home for Christmas.

Christmas smelled like pine needles; our tree was put up Christmas Eve, but I had to wait until evening before I could go into the dining room to see it. My mother told me that the *Christkind* was decorating the tree. When I finally came into the room, candles on the tall fir tree were lighted and my father stood beside it. He reflected the warm light from the candles. He smiled at me. It was his Christmas, he had done it for me, he loved me and wanted me to be happy. My father still stands there in the candlelight and smiles in anticipation of my reaction to the candlelight and smiles in anticipation of my reaction to the presents. It was the last time a man wooed me with a Christmas of my own, and with presents nearly impossible to come by during the war: a tractor that sent out red flames through its exhaust pipe, a tank that made noises and flames through the gun turrets, and a Ju-88, a Stuka, in camouflage colors. But it was a castle that seduced me forever. It stood on a small mountain, crags covered with painted snow. It had a drawbridge, a tall and a small tower, gates, a courtyard surrounded by walls and a big building. When I came into the room, I saw a soft glow coming from the castle's windows. A small battery and a light bulb inside the building lit the house. The roofs of the towers, gates, and building glittered under the illusion of snow; the light from the castle threw shadows across the courtyard.

My castle stood next to the nativity scene my father had built. He had carved all the animals; only Joseph, Mary, and Jesus were bought. The two miniature worlds were halfway stuck in the low branches of the fir tree. The branches surrounded them like forests; in the soft shadows of the candlelight, the castle and the nativity scene looked calm and warm; my father had created them, he had given me my own domain to rule, the two worlds were secure. I wanted to reduce myself to their scale and live in them, beautiful islands floating on the scented breezes of pine and heated wax. My father had given me a world to live in, self-contained, and enclosed by turrets and moats.

The picture my father shot the following day shows me surrounded by toys. I am squatting on the floor, my toys arranged around the castle, my father's son.

Another flickering memory from that Christmas Eve 1942. After we had opened our presents we went downstairs to the office where the apple gendarme was on duty. We lit candles and sang Christmas songs. Candlelight threw a soft glimmer over Hitler's sepia picture. While we wished each other "Fröliche Weihnachten," I thought of my castle upstairs.

•   •   •

Shortly after Christmas there was heavy snow. Gertrude and I took our sled that had the word *Vorwärts* burned into it and went zooming down the hill in front of our old monastery. We watched our parents and Frau Ritter hide with big buckets of snow at the upstairs windows and dump them on Herr Ritter as he came in the front door. He grabbed a handful of snow and rushed upstairs after them. Their laughter and screams rang through the house as they fled through the corridors.

Snow and heavy gray skies that reached the ground surrounded the gendarmerie. The snow muffled all sounds in the garden where Irmtraud and I were building snowmen, while the apple gendarme shouted advice to us from the office window. Gertrude chased crows out of the pear tree because they ate the sunflower seeds she had put out for the small birds. It was a perfect world. In the evening we sat in our warm kitchen and listened to the humming radio. The outside world was something else. Far beyond our kitchen and the protective snow clouds, Churchill and Roosevelt had met in Casablanca and announced they would accept nothing but Germany's unconditional surrender. I was sleepy and listened to the words our *Telefunken* had mysteriously gleaned from the air and funneled into our kitchen. My parents listened silently; my mother as usual shook her head. At the end of January, the radio announced that Stalingrad had fallen to the Russians. Frau Ritter came upstairs and put her hands up in the air and said: "Our poor boys! What is going to become of them in all that Russian snow and ice?" My mother as usual answered: "What a world! Where is it going to end?"

• • •

I was the apple of my father's eye. He was constantly telling my mother not to let anything happen to me. She was always poking her head out of windows to check up on me, or peering around corners to monitor me on Linden Square. She was mortified when shortly when shortly after the fall of Stalingrad I was buried over my head by snow that had fallen from the gendarmerie roof. Warm weather had loosened the heavy snow. I was just pulling my sled up the hill when I heard a sliding sound above me. It hit me on the head and within seconds absorbed me. Daylight came through a wet, white filter. Snow clogged my mouth and I couldn't move.

One second I had been on the hill with other children, the next I had vanished. Muffled sounds came through the snow. I inhaled snow through my nostrils. I was petrified, and felt I was going to die and dissolve into the cold, white substance. I was alone. I wanted to scream but only snow turned in my mouth.

Gertrude and the other children dug out my head from the snow but two gendarmes had to come down from the office and get the rest with shovels, because I was impacted in the snow. The kids stood around me, laughed and sang: "Winfried got stuck in the snow, Winfried got stuck in the snow…!" I felt tears of rage well up but I didn't cry. Something terrible had happened but the world thought it was funny. There was no way of telling them how it felt being inside the avalanche.

▧17▧

According to the moves of history, the gendarmes' map of the larger Germany was no longer correct. On it the red-shaded areas still went beyond Stalingrad, because the gendarmes had used permanent ink. The apple gendarme told me our retreat was only temporary and I believed him — the headlines in the *Völkischer Beobachter* said the same, I could read them myself. Sometimes around St. Nikolaus and my father's magic castle, I had settled down to decipher words in the papers. It was German history that urged me on to decode the mystery of words and letter combinations.

The war was my primer. The red and black headlines of the *Völkischer Beobachter* and the ordinary print of our local paper interpreted the war for me. Stalingrad falls! The Luftwaffe bombs London! The drama of London was bigger though less intense than Stalingrad. German fighters shoot up RAF! That line was more personalized; I could envision individual Germans involved in the fight. But in general, they were reduced to words that embodied "us" or "them." The shape of "London" in particular was dark and dangerous. The word had two eyes that never closed; the sound of the word made two explosions. The RAF came from there. They came at night. They were invisible machines high in the air, from London. I became particularly fascinated by the RAF when one morning, after an air alert, we found leaflets and mysterious strips of aluminum in our garden. I stared at the leaflet: a screaming Hitler with his hands in the air was standing over a bloody map of Europe. Irmtraud's mother said we had to bring it right away to the office because it was illegal to keep enemy leaflets. It made the piece of paper that had dropped out of the skies even more magical. It came from the other side, from "them," from London! They had been here, invisible during the night! We wondered if it was poisoned.

We asked the gendarmes about the silvery foil. They told us it was dropped by the enemy to confuse our radar. We were allowed to keep them and stored the foil in our tree house where we looked at it as evidence from an alien world. We sniffed them, but they gave off no English smell.

I wondered if Wellingtons or Lancasters had dropped the foil and leaflets. Maybe it was a Short Sterling Mk? I knew all the aircraft, German and Allied. My speculations were well-founded in facts. Wolfram had given me a large colored map of friendly and hostile planes, and my father had pinned it to the wall above my bed, directly across from our madonna. I could match frontal and side views with the correct type of aircraft. Before I went to sleep, and in the morning before I got up, I studied the map. Fighters and heavy bombers. Germany didn't have four-engine bombers, but the Allies did; four-engine bombers were my favorites.

I could spell B-17, Lancaster, Wellington, Handley-Page, and Condor by heart. Their silhouettes hovered before my eyes after the light was turned off. The letter and number combinations were like mystic symbol: He-111, B-24, Me-109, Spitfire, Ju-87, Focke-Wulf 189A; I wrote them on paper. I liked bombers that were bulky in front and diminishing at the tail end. I concentrated my eyes on the B-17, but I never told Wolfram how I liked that American bomber. The B-17 was a silvery-blue body that floated inexorably toward its goal. Its four powerful engines seduced me.

• • •

While I increased the radius of my solitary reading skills, the chestnut and linden trees started to turn green. We watched Frau Beyer plant marigolds in her garden. My mother said she loved a variety of marigolds called "student flowers" in German. She broke off a leaf and smelled it. "Ah" she said, "it's an herb, stringent and pure, it cleans out your nose!" I smelled one and agreed. The flower reminded me of the apprentices in Herr Heim's shop, because they were students too. I held the leaf in front of Irmtraud's nose. She screamed and said "Pfui! It stinks!" But I had discovered something new. I kept going over to Frau Beyer's flower beds and smelling *Studentenblumen* that spring until Frau Beyer told me to stop ruining her marigolds.

At the same time I discovered marigolds, the RAF bombed the Möhne-Eder dams with Lancasters and gigantic bombs. At the end of May, a thousand bombers attacked Cologne. I looked at my plane chart more carefully at night before I went to sleep. Irmtraud and I discussed bombers and air-raid shelters. She assured me that we were too far away to be bombed, and we went back to our teas in the tree. But our marriage began to show strain.

One day, a relative of the Röhmers who was also a friend of my mother came to visit. She brought us half a pound of butter and smuggled it upstairs. I was told not to say anything to the Röhmers and went straight down to tell them. Frau Röhmer stopped speaking to my mother who offered the butter to her. Irmtraud and I didn't play with each other for a few days; our mothers made up, but I blushed every time the word butter was mentioned in my presence.

My father went back to the Black Forest to complete his officer's training, and my mother and I went for a visit in Würzburg.

≋18≋

My Aunt Anna, while pointing at me, always said that I had trains and planes on the brain. "Mark my words!" she said, "He isn't going to stay long in one place when he's grown up! Remember, he wanted to take the train to Bamberg with his rubber sheet when he wasn't even three!" Her eyes were a little cross-eyed as she looked at me from the side and shook her head.

Aunt Anna was right. In the Spring of 1943 I was willing to abandon Irmtraud and the gendarmerie for any train ride; but we didn't go very far that spring, we only went to Münnerstadt. Though it wasn't more than 60 miles it took three hours on a local with a change of trains at Schweinfurt. The length of the trip made up for the shortness of the distance.

Shortly before we left for Münnerstadt, my father had come back for a vacation form Freiburg. He was tanned from skiing in the Black Forest and could speak some Russian he had learned in a crash course. We looked at him with open mouths as he spoke the language of the people who had taken Stalingrad from us. My puzzled mother asked him why he had taken Russian? What good would it do for a gendarme in Franconia?

Before he returned to Freiburg, my father brought Gertrude, my mother, and me to the station to catch the morning train. It arrived on platform one. It had Kitzingen-Schweinfurt, via Gerolzhofen written on signs along the sides of the carriages. Gertrude said this train went as fast as a cow, but I didn't listen. I didn't want to disappoint myself; I was going to Istanbul or to Cairo to link up with our desert corps and Field Marshal Rommel. I didn't know that he was about to capitulate to the Allies. I hadn't learned yet to read between the lines of the *Völkischer Beobachter*.

A small, sooty black locomotive had been hitched to our train with its front. It pulled backwards; the pointed cow-catcher faced in the wrong direction, and this bothered me. Nobody could tell me why locomotives were sometimes turned around. I had to ignore it so as not to spoil my trip to Istanbul. All the way through the soft hills and valleys of Northern Franconia, I stood at the windows and watched the

Balkans go by. Gertude and I had once traced the route of the Orient Express on her green atlas. Loudspeakers announced "Winfried en route to Constantinople" at all stations. The world watched me rush by in steam and soot via Belgrade toward the Greek border. German troops were at all the stations; the ride went through solid German territory. Swastikas and officers waved to me from strange foreign stations, bands played, farmers stood silently along the route to catch a glimpse of my flashing eyes that zipped by with the speed of light. They were dazzled by the express that came from the depth of the German Reich and steamed toward the glittering minarets of Byzantium.

In Schweinfurt, my fantasy came to an end. I saw the first bombed buildings of my life. The section around the station had been hit: black facades with nothing behind them. Gertrude said it was because of the ball bearing plants; my mother pointed to some of the ruins and said she couldn't believe all this — the Schweinfurt she knew so well had disappeared! While we sat on a bench waiting for our connection the sirens went off. Panic broke out around us while we sat paralyzed on our bench. People ran past us screaming. It was a clear and sunny day, and the Americans were coming to hit the plants again. A conductor shouted at us to go to the bunker outside the station; we took our suitcase and ran after the others.

The bunker was four stories high, solid gray concrete, a gigantic cube with small ventilation slits. A big crowd was surging toward the entrance, and my mother cried: "Why did we have to change trains in Schweinfurt today...?" But nobody answered her. A man screamed, "Women and children first!" My mother yanked up my arm in the direction of the voice and shouted, "Here! Here! I have a little boy with me!" I got inside the bunker before the others, but felt embarrassed while we pushed through the waiting crowd. An old man said, *"So'n kleiner Verrecker, warum soll der vor uns reinkommen?"* "That little son-of-a-bitch, why should he get in before us?" I had never been called a son-of-a-bitch. I turned fiery red as my mother and Gertrude pulled me into the dark bunker. The sun was blotted out.

Inside it was stale and humid. Weak bulbs burned along the walls. We sat on a wooden bench and waited. Outside, the anti-aircraft guns thundered. A woman with a scarf around her head sat next to us. She had a little boy too. I wondered if he was also a son-of-a-bitch. The woman said that every time the weather was nice she and her little boy went straight to the bunker early in the morning to make sure they got in. She wasn't going to take any chances. My mother said: "We are lucky in Kitzingen, we don't have much industry…" The American B-17 stayed away that day; only a few enemy planes flew over the city and the all-clear signal let us out. We went back to the station where we took the train to Münnerstadt.

•   •   •

Instead of Constantinople I arrived at Münnerstadt in Upper Franconia, where we stayed with my Aunt Dorothea who always said in her Franconian dialect *"Mach' doch kei Pförz,"* "Don't make any farts," which meant "Don't be an asshole."

My aunt lived on the big square across from the Dominicans who brewed beer and ran a boys' school. But I never saw them and quickly got bored in Münnerstadt once the train ride through the Balkans had worn off. But I was secure in my Aunt's house which, as a historical monument had to be kept scrupulously clean on the outside. It was constantly being whitewashed and had lace curtains behind the windows and red geraniums in front. Inside, the house was a jumble of dark, irregular rooms that hadn't been renovated since the eighteenth century, crumbling staircases, which were oiled occasionally, and creaking, winding corridors.

On the first floor was my aunt's grocery store, her living room, and a huge kitchen with twenty-foot ceilings. A window opened into a dark, drafty alley frequented by rats. My Uncle Adam, an ardent hunter, often sat at the open window with a gun and shot rats. He also killed hamsters. During the war he dressed up the rats and hamsters as rabbit and sold it for stew across my aunt's counter. "Meat is meat," he said, "and war is war!"

Münnerstadt was too small to be bombed. The people didn't bother with shelters when the sirens sounded. Two days after our arrival, huge fleets of silvery B-17s appeared in the blue sky. The planes were divided into box-like formations, emitting hundreds of contrails that clouded the skies. Everybody stood on the street and watched the Americans overhead, shading their eyes with hands, guessing where the planes were going. My mother said, "Those poor people who are going to get it today!" I stood on a large can of cranberry preserves so I could lean out of my aunt's window. The lid caved in and I fell into the preserves with my dirty boots. My aunt's daughter screamed "Holy Mary and Joseph! If my mother finds out she'll kill us; there are no more cranberries in all Franconia!" While the ominous enemy fleets roared overhead, we cleaned my boots of the sticky preserves and closed the lid carefully. My aunt sold the cranberries a few days later.

I watched Uncle Adam with fascination and disgust as he

sat at the dreary kitchen window with his gun. We weren't allowed to make any noise. Some rats turned somersaults when they got hit, some just squealed and rolled over. After he killed a rat, Uncle Adam reloaded his gun, then climbed out of the window and picked up the rat by its tail. When he climbed back into the kitchen with a rat, Gertrude screamed and ran off into my aunt's store.

Uncle Adam only shot rats when he was bored and had nothing else to shoot. He often hunted in the forests and stayed at a small lodge not far from Münnerstadt. It was whispered that he often took strange women to the lodge and gave them presents. I heard Aunt Anna say he bought a fur coat on the black market for one of his whores. Although I didn't know what a whore was, I imagined a woman covered from head to toe in dirt and excrement. I also heard it whispered that Uncle Adam shot deer beyond his quota; and that was dangerous. Field Marshall Göring himself had made German hunting laws the strictest in the world. Whenever Uncle Adam shot more than he was allowed, the deer was hung in the cold, white-tiled room off the big hall. The room was kept locked. The venison was sold on the black market.

One day Uncle Adam took me into the cold room and showed me how he cleaned a deer. A carcass was hanging from a hook. He cut into the hide at various spots and told me to pull. The animal smelled much like dead leaves in the forest and was ice cold. I didn't want to pull. So my uncle pulled the skin over the animal's head. The dead eyes of the animal were bulging out of the skinless body like two big marbles. I thought they would burst.

Uncle Adam showed me another carcass hanging from the ceiling. He told me to take a good look while he pulled the haunches open. Tiny white worms were crawling in the carcass. They looked like my own worms, but unlike mine, these made me shudder. Death was a wriggling mass of tiny white forms. I took a step backwards. "Hmm," Uncle Adam said, "the meat is tender for stew now!" but later, when my Aunt served the stew, we didn't eat. My aunt got angry and said we didn't know what we missed, we hadn't starved enough, yet, and she said: *"Macht doch kei Pförz! Esst!"* We only shook our heads. She got even angrier, when one evening, she served us strong Limburger and boiled potatoes with butter. Gertrude didn't eat butter; and when Tante Dorothea tried to force butter and Limburger down her throat, Gertrude fainted and rolled off her chair. She stared at the contorted eyes of my sister and said: "You're all crazy! You deserve to starve to death!"

🔊19🔊

While Uncle Adam shot rats in the kitchen alley, our Afrika Korps fought with its back to the sea. Tunis and Bizerte were words that floated out from my aunt and uncle's radio next to the telephone each evening. While we ate Aunt Dorothea's boiled potatoes and green salad, the announcer informed us that the Germans were fighting heroically to the last man. I had the habit of sitting on my left leg when I ate; my aunt told my mother that this wasn't a proper way for a boy to eat, and I had to put my leg down.

We stayed on in Münnerstadt where the food was good. News from north Africa alternated with news from Warsaw, and my aunt minded her store selling flowers and vegetables, surrounded by the smells that centuries had given her house: old mortar, rotting beams, humid corridors, dry goods, flowers, vanilla, drying animal skins, the maid's cooking, barrels of pickles and sauerkraut, and detergents. And, on warm days, there were strong odors arising from Aunt Dorothea's toilets.

She had two of them. My Aunt Augusta from the north called them *"Plumpsklos,"* "plop-johns," because everything fell straight down into a black hole. There was no clear, swirling water that gurgled over shiny, porcelain bowls, licking every inch with a satisfying sucking noise before it vanished in the opening. Tante Dorothea only had black holes that led into a void.

One toilet was on the ground floor off the big hall. I had to climb up four rickety steps that led into a small cabinet with a dreary light bulb hanging form the ceiling. There was just enough space to sit down on a wooden bench, shiny and smooth from use, and the wooden, whitewashed door was right in front of my nose. Through the cracks, I could see people come into the hall and buy vegetables and flowers. I always waited until everybody had gone, before I came out.

Aunt Dorothea had a round lid on the opening of the toilet. Whenever I pulled it out by the knob, the lid made a sound like a gigantic cork being pulled from a bottle; while I looked for a place for the lid, the past of my uncle, my aunt, and her daughter rose from the hole and filled every inch of the little room. A sharp, bitter smell like forests of mushrooms rotting in the wet dark.

The other toilet was on the second floor off the main corridor. It didn't even have a door. I was told to shout when I heard someone coming upstairs. The difference between the downstairs and the upstairs toilets was that the whole upstairs was brightly lit by the sun during the day. It went straight down into a hidden courtyard that served four adjoining houses. I always thought of those four houses backing into the courtyard with their rear ends, crouching like humans in a state of perpetual defecation.

While sitting on the upstairs hole, I could look down and see the discharged me hit the yard two stories below and disintegrate with soft sputtering explosions. I was a B-17 bombing the world; I had long-range gas tanks and could reach Singapore. The hole was big enough for me to fall through, and I had been warned always to lean forward. I could strain my head backward and see the court below in different kinds of light according to the time of day. Below me surged a malleable, dark sea of varying browns and dark yellows across the yard. Wavelets of green licked the outer fringes. Currents of reds, the color of toadstools, flowed through the massive browns. Here and there appeared crests of decaying white, like white caps on a dark sea. Thus I studied internal history, my aunt's and uncle's secret life. While back in Münnerstadt, I thus fell back into the mystic stages of my soul.

I was intrigued with the upstairs toilet. On warm, sunny days, I sat endlessly on the second floor seat next to stacks of the *Völkischer Beobacter*, which we used for toilet paper, and stared below at new topographies every day. I began to recreate all the continents and countries that were in my sister's atlas, just as I had done in Kitzingen before Ilse discovered me, and, while I listened to the sounds of the past three hundred years of my aunt's house creak around me, I watched the world below. It was alive with a million shiny wings of flies during the spring of 1943.

111

The flies were called *Schmeissfliegen*, appropriately, I thought, because *Schmeiss* rhymed with *Scheiss*, the German word for shit. The heavy blowflies banged against Aunt Dorothea's whitewashed walls as if they were bent on suicide. Sometimes they clung with a humming sound on the rough stone, roughly rubbing their legs over their wings and head. I imagined that they were cleaning themselves from the brown mire below.

I watched them from my high seat expecting them to leave a trail of brown spots when they walked across the walls. They had sucked the fermenting juices until they looked too heavy to fly. They were bomb-loaded He-111s ready to take off for London. They taxied on runways, flew off to bomb the enemy.

The blowflies also carried diseases; my mother had said. So I turned them into Lancasters that had to be shot down before they reached the Reich. They were infectious machines filled with brown phosphor to set our cities on fire. I tried to flatten them with double layers of newspaper. A Lancaster, when smashed with a direct hit, became a large black crater with red and white spots. The black and red print of *Völkischer Beobacter* smudged the white walls and surrounded the high-flying cameras of our Intelligence Bureau recording victories of the Luftwaffe. I kept careful score. I oversaw the hectic activities on friendly and hostile airfields that readied armadas of bombers and fighters against each other. Aunt Dorothea, who told the maid downstairs what to cook for lunch, had no idea what was going on in her house one flight up. While she cooked, an apocalypse took place upstairs.

Aunt Dorothea always laughed at us because we washed our hands as soon as we came in from the toilet. She said we were too hygienic, that we washed our natural resistances away. *"Das ist nicht gut!"* she said.

All the hunters and forest rangers who visited my uncle never washed their hands either. On rainy days they smelled like their wet dogs. The smell sat in their heavy loden coats. They drank schnapps, toasted their hunting, the Führer, whose photograph hung over the radio next to Jesus on a small cross with a black rosary wrapped around it. On the other wall, my aunt had a colored picture of the Virgin and a painting with a leaping buck in the middle of a forest.

I didn't like my uncle's friends. It was reciprocal. They were old, not like the apprentices in Herr Heim's shop. I didn't understand their jokes; they talked about girls in hunting lodges...ha ha ha! My uncle claimed that no woman had ever been disappointed by him! He smoothed his black moustache as he spoke.

Aunt Anna was always saying that Uncle Adam wasn't normal anymore. They would have to put a girl in his coffin when he died. The image of a young girl being forced into a coffin with my dead uncle scared me. It reminded me of the neat churchyard in Münnerstadt where my mother and Aunt Dorothea would go in the afternoons to see who was lying in coffins in the little chapel. When I came with them, I saw old men and women with pale faces and pinched mouths and thin noses pointing upwards like those of Herr Kolb and Herr Nüsslein, lying in narrow coffins with the smell of wilting flowers. The corpses came to haunt me at night when I went to the toilet on the second floor. I carried a candle because there was no electricity in the corridors and no chamber pots for our rooms. I would have died on the spot if the candle had gone out. I was sure that some night I would find one of the corpses, or my dead grandmother, who had died on the second floor, sitting on the toilet when I came around the corner.

• • •

The same time our army capitulated in north Africa, I developed a fear of the dark in Aunt Dorothea's house. During the day everything was fine and bright; but as soon as the sun went down, I was startled by every sound her house made. When I passed the locked rooms on the second floor at night, where my aunt kept antique furniture and coin collections, I had the feeling the locked doors would suddenly fly open and I would be sucked into dark spaces. I put my mother between me and the dark. I made her carry the candles and watched the shadows dance against the walls. When my aunt heard about my fears, she called me *"einen kleinen Angstscheisser,"* "a small fear-shitter." I didn't care what she said. At night I could hear her house breathe, especially the abandoned third floor with its empty rooms. The house had nightmares, it groaned, it opened and closed its eyes, as wind whistled through its empty spaces and through the open toilet seat. Mice scurried on the third floor where humid odors emanated.

• • •

Every afternoon we had coffee in the living room. Gertrude and I had to make sure all doors and windows were closed so the odor of coffee wouldn't escape. My aunt didn't want anybody to know she still had real coffee.

I sat under the leaping buck and heard the maid whip cream in the kitchen. "Hm," my mother said, "I hope you appreciate that! There won't be any of this in Kitzingen!" Everything smelled warm, comfortable and secure. My aunt had baked a *Gügelhupf* with powdered sugar on top. "It's a pre-war cake," she said. All the adults spoke of pre-war and war-quality. The pre-war era was a mythic time when I had been hardly conscious. The cake dissolved into fine fragrant crumbs on my tongue. My sister Gertrude whispered into my mother's ears loud enough that my aunt who sat on the couch could hear. Gertrude said Uncle Adam had offered her five marks in the hall if she would give him a kiss! I kept eating my cake while my mother stared at Gertrude, holding her fork in the air. My aunt quietly got up and went into the hall. "Oh," the maid said, "you shouldn't have said that…" Gertrude shook herself in disgust and said she had lost her appetite for cake and coffee; a terrible scream came form the hall. The maid wagged her index finger at my sister and we all ran out to see. Boxes and crates were upside down in the big hall and my aunt was chasing Uncle Adam with an ax.

Aunt Dorothea held the ax high above her head and screamed a word I had never heard before: "*Du Hürenbock!*" "You whoring old buck." We stood at the door stretching our necks like three cranes, ready to duck back into the living room. The maid went after my aunt and tried to get the ax away form her; my uncle's dog was nipping my aunt's leg. My mother called out "Dorothea!" but she didn't seem to hear. My uncle ran into the toilet and locked the door. My aunt buried the ax with a hollow thud into the door then sat down on a crate and cried.

We left the next day. My aunt didn't speak to anyone, my uncle had gone off to the forest. We went back to Kitzingen via Bad Kissingen and Würzburg to make sure that we wouldn't get bombed by the Americans while changing trains in Schweinfurt.

☙20❧

The German Reich knew the dangerous effects that films could have on the young and on principle prohibited most films for anyone under eighteen. But I was allowed to see historical epics, propaganda films, and light entertainment that couldn't corrupt my Aryan spirit. I loved films and begged my parents to take me to the movies even though they weren't allowed to. I thought the adults could somehow smuggle me into the movie house, but they wouldn't. I felt cheated, I was enraged. Films were in my blood.

By the summer of 1943 I was hooked. Every Wednesday afternoon I waited upstairs on the landing for the local newspaper to be delivered. Films changed on Wednesdays and our two theaters ran their ads. I rushed downstairs and opened to the ad section with trembling hands. I could read titles; they were either above or below the pictures: men and women close to each other in some languorous embrace, with shocking events displayed behind them. Underneath were the film companies' names and logos: Terra, Bavaria, UFA, I knew them all. With a thumping heart I looked for the words *Jugendfrei*, which included me, or *Für Jugendliche verboten!* Which shut me out. I saw *Stuka, Achtung! Feind hört mit, U-Boot, Friedrich der Grosse*, and then I made a fateful acquaintance in the dark warm womb of the movies: Zarah Leander.

She had made two films I was allowed to see, *Fronttheatre*

and *Die Grosse Liebe*. In both she had long eyelashes, dark liquid eyes, (always filling with tears of longing), and she sang in the low voice that made her famous. Gertrude collected photographs of film stars and had many of Zarah. People spoke of her in hushed tones, and in musical numbers choruses of girls in white dresses moved their arms up and down and breathed sounds in the background. I saw one of her films twice; once with Gertrude in the afternoon and once with my parents at night. They sneaked me into the theatre although children weren't allowed. I was so excited that my bladder got nervous. We stood in the foyer and I remember officers going by. Inside the theater lights went out, a gong sounded as the curtain parted, then came the ads, and then the *Deutsche Wochenschau*, the newsreel. An eagle was entwined with a swastika and lights behind it went up and down…the German Army was advancing, and planes bombed a city. Then: *Zarah*.

The movies were a self-contained world, that nothing could disrupt. It was safe, warm, enclosed, and Zarah Leander performed a melodrama that didn't require thinking. In following her actions and words, one followed truth. She nearly pulled my eyes from their sockets as they followed her across the black and white screen. My very soul adored her longing eyes as she sang *"Der Wind hat mir ein Lied erzählt,"* and *"Ich weiss, es wird einmal ein Wünder geschehen."* In one song, she was listening to the wind telling her something through the subtle voice of nature, while in the other, she was yearning for a miracle: the right man. Zarah Leander just stood there, waiting.

I began to reenact Leander-drama in our living room. I smuggled a veil into the empty room and draped it around me. Then, in a low voice I sang Zarah. I went into the *ich-*

weiss-eswird-einmal-ein-Wünder-geschehen routine. I swirled and bowed, I gazed out windows into the distance, past the smoke stack of the municipal hospital. Our old yellow monastery expanded, the polished floor receded, I no longer knew where I was. I could have been anywhere where Zarah had been: the steppes of Hungary, or Russia, at the front, in the vast sky. The Leander in my soul opened like an exotic flower, I reveled in the Leander-me, turning to the tunes of my own orchestra. I was the center; I languished, and waited for the miracle to happen. So it went, performance after performance, by myself, in our quiet living room... until, one day, my sister Gertrude watched me through the keyhole. She ran to get my mother and they peered through the keyhole watching me do Zarah Leander. Later on, they said they nearly died with laughter; they had to put their handkerchiefs over their mouths to keep from exploding. They took turns imitating me imitating Leander to their friends. Then Gertrude finally burst into the room triumphantly shouting that they had seen EVERYTHING! My act folded. My tiny Leander-self shriveled back into its mystic shell. After a moment of existential embarrassment, I took a kick at Gertrude's shins.

My Leander act became a big story for anyone who wanted to hear it. Every time we had visitors I cringed because I knew they would hear about it. Then everyone would laugh, look at me, and start singing Leander. I had been exposed. I was too cute to be believed. As soon as I heard the name Zarah Leander, I turned crimson. I was asked to give public performances. I refused; I was even offered money, first twenty-five pfennig then up to fifty. I still shook my head. One day, an old friend of my mother, visiting form Münnerstadt where she had a hat shop, went as high as one mark. "Come on my little Winfried," she said as she held the mark up for me to see, "Come on, do it for me!" I refused again.

I looked at them morosely when they said I was a born actor. I wonder where he got it from, they asked themselves. But I wasn't an actor, otherwise I would have taken the money. I couldn't repeat the act publicly because it was a non-public act. I was Leander, and they didn't understand.

• • •

The impact of the movies is evident in our photo album. In snapshots of that time I'm looking at the world with a coy Leander-look... "Come and get me," I'm signaling, "I'm here!" I posed for frontal shots with my eyes lowered, I looked at the world from below, my head slightly turned aside. I'm flirting with the entire world; one leg posed before the other, I always had my left hand in my pocket with the thumb always outside the pocket. The thumb looks self-conscious (maybe Gertrude advised me on posing), as if I were tempting the world with my thumb. So it went in picture after picture-along the Main River, before the Art Nouveau Luitpoldbad, in the park, in front of the railway station-everywhere, I had veiled Zarah eyes inviting the world to me.

21

Meanwhile, the Axis went downhill. Wolfram said our setbacks were only temporary and we would soon recover our old drive. We had the best army in the world, the best generals, and, most of all, we had Hitler.

It was Spring 1943. As usual the chestnuts bloomed. First, they had swollen buds with sweet sticky drops that tempted me to climb into the trees. Soon, white blossoms unfurled to produce little green spiked balls that eventually became chestnuts. The linden trees on the square turned a deep green, leaving a slight scent of blossoms in the air. I played with Irmtraud in the pear tree; she served tea, she was my wife; we spanked our child, her big doll, because Irmtraud said our child didn't want to play the piano.

My father came back from Freiburg in his black boots and green uniform. He was my familiar father. He hadn't changed. The shape and scent of his body (cigarettes and a faint smell of sweat) embraced me constantly, and I clung to them unconsciously for protection. It never occurred to me that it could end, that my father's green uniform could walk out of the gendarmerie and never return. He was eternally fixed in his path between the gendarmerie and the country-side like a constellation in the sky. He left us to enforce the law on the outside, but always returned to us who relied on him. My mother was always saying "Let's wait and see what father thinks..."or "That's a man's job..." and then my father would do whatever was necessary, making us both secure.

I wasn't aware that the blue smoke of his Russian ciga-rettes wouldn't always curl out of the office window behind the vines; that his presence, his gestures and motions were limited in time, that my father was about to pass from my view into territories where he couldn't take me.

One day in July, while Irmtraud and I sat in our pear tree, an officer rang our bell. Since my father was out getting a haircut, there is no record of how he would have confronted the news. But my mother cried at once when the officer told her, that since he was a personal friend of my father, he had wanted to tell him himself that my father had been ordered to go to Russia in August. Russia! My mother cried at once, Russia was doom and destruction! *Russland!* And she repeated that my father had chronic bronchitis, and that he had been already at the front in the first war. The Russian winter would be the worst thing for his bronchitis.

I had come down from the pear tree and listened to adults in the living room that was reserved for Christmas and special occasions. The SS-officer nodded his head sympathetically when my mother said this wasn't fair, they couldn't do this to us. The officer shrugged his shoulders apologetically; my mother offered him a glass of schnapps and he lit a cigarette. He shook my hand and patted my head. "You will have to look after your mother now," he said. "You'll be the man in the house!" Then he looked around surreptitiously, and under his breath told my mother that my father wasn't scheduled to go to Russia initially, but that he had to take the place of a colleague who had bribed his way out. But this was very secret information!

The officer's privileged information occupied us day and night. It wasn't fate that was against us, it was injustice perpetrated by someone who posed as a friend. My father was calm and stoic; he said this was the way it was there was nothing to be done. But my mother dug and chiseled away at the information trying to find out who had bribed himself out of Russia and doomed my father. We were victims of injustice, protesting at headquarters.

My father's trip to Würzburg brought my idyllic marriage to Irmtraud to an end; it had been *her* father who bribed his way out of the Russian front! My father's friends at headquarters told him the truth; but nothing could be done about it, my father had to go. Bitterly my mother recalled that Frau Röhmer had said a few months earlier that she would do anything and pull any strings to get her husband off in case he had to go the front. "Well," my mother said, "she succeeded; she has connections but we don't!" Our closest colleague had betrayed us from within our own gendarmerie!

Through all the commotion I recall my father's quiet resignation. Later on, my mother always repeated: "My husband was an honest man, he did what he was told, he did his duty, he had integrity, he couldn't stand trying to back out of things, and what did he get for it?" My father was an honest man, a tragic figure! We were victims. My mother said, "They think they can do anything with a woman whose husband could be crushed like a twig." As an extension of my mother I was a victim too. Widow and half-orphan, the two of us united by the conspiracy of evil. My mother created herself and me in a melodrama: victims waiting passively for the next assault. With my father gone, our protection was removed and the icy dark winds were blowing through our old monastery.

In July 1943 my Agfa-marriage with Irmtraud dissolved. Though I was allowed to play with her as before ("Let's keep the children out of this…"), I saw Irmtraud as her father's daughter. Every time I saw her, her father's terrible betrayal sat on her forehead. She was guilty of his crime. We stopped our teas in the pear tree; she gave more time to her piano, and I contemplated my carpenter-apprentice at my leisure. My mother strode icily past Frau Röhmer who withered under my mother's glacial *"Güten Tag."*

"God will take care of them, they'll get theirs," my mother said, and "God's mills grind slow but fine…" It was one of the few times that I had heard my mother refer to God as an intervening cause. Frau Röhmer on the other hand tried to soothe her conscience by sending baskets of plums and apples to us, fresh from her trees. We sent them back without comment. To avoid further embarrassment, the Röhmers asked for a quick transfer and with their good connections they got it at once.

Irmtaud was to go out of my life! She became a soft glow of my childhood, a radiating light from which emanated my own innocence. She left behind a series of photographs shot through with smiles, black and white spring mornings, over-exposed skies, light gray afternoons, blurred moments that tried to capture us "as we were" for the future with a shutter speed that was too slow. Our childhood is framed by lilacs, blooming hawthorn, chestnut trees, linden trees, daisies, and dandelions. They spread their innocence around us, we lived in the poetic backdrop our parents had lovingly chosen for us as if they could influence our future lives. The "look-at-them" and "Aren't-they-too-cute-for-words!" — flashes of our past on grainy Afga-Lupex paper remain of what once was and never was, what one wishes it to be, what childhood was supposed to be in the eyes of the amateur photographers as they released the shutter: childhood went on in spite of history around us. We, Irmtraud and I, are the ones that matter.

℞22℟

August 1, 1943. In a daring long-range attack, the Americans bombed the oil fields of Ploesti to destroy our resources. We walked my father to the station as if we were out on a Sunday stroll, as if nothing was happening. Up the Landwehrstrasse, through the square arch of the Neue Brücke, up the hill, along the old chestnut trees of the Adolf Hitler Strasse that lead right into the railway station. We are out on the platform with him. It is a sunny day; my mother quietly cries and dabs her eyes. "Don't worry," my father is saying, "I'll be back in three months, it's promised!" To me he says, "be a good student this fall." The train arrives on platform number three. My father gets into a second-class compartment and comes back out to embrace us once more; the conductor shoves him gently back in. The train moves out in the direction of Nürnberg, east, in big puffs of smoke. Slow at first, it moves faster and faster until my father who is leaning out of the window and waving a white handkerchief is so small that my eyes no longer can make out. And, thus my father, his gendarme-green aura in black boots disappeared from my life in clouds of black smoke.

I can't remember if I was sad. My mother tells me I asked when Dad would be coming back. I take her word for it. I remember looking out the window that afternoon and seeing my mother sitting on an upturned crate in the Beyers' part of the garden holding a handkerchief in front in front of her eyes. She is immovable, unaware her son is watching from above.

§23§

My father: my life's mystery. He became a model on which I was supposed to form myself. But his absence made it impossible. He became a metaphor. Whenever things went wrong, his memory was there to remind us of past times when his presence guaranteed the smooth order of things. His was the just and honest age; his absence encouraged chaos. I vaguely felt I should do something about it, since I was his only son; but it quickly disappeared and made way for the notion that our present lamentable state was a natural one; there was little I could do, we could only pray for the best. My mother said so.

My father adored writing the capital letters M and W in his signature. The letters start on the left, sweep upwards like an act of elegant courage, turn to the right and downward only to sweep upward again. They fix his presence forever in space; self-assured masculine penmanship in Sütterlin-Schrift, the old German alphabet. His signature is a legacy putting me to shame with its sheer beauty and power. Bold strokes going out into the world. Firmly anchored black boots, essence of strict green. Who was this man, who — as my mother said after the collapse — didn't do anything except escort the Jews to the railway station? I don't know.

Between August 1 and November 20,1943, my father wrote thirty letters and seven cards to us from Russia. Whenever he could he wrote us. He typed his letters, used ink, pencils, on any kind of paper he could find. Often his letters were held up and arrived weeks later; he received ours sometimes in five days, sometimes they took two weeks. He wrote sitting on his cot, at a desk in the Ukraine, in a car somewhere out in the vast Russian steppes covered with dust. He tried to ward off the vastness of Russia with a kind of magic charm: he was counting days until he could return. Each letter recorded the number of days left at the bottom. He won't expand on his adventures in Russia because he wants to tell us everything himself…a guarantee that he will come back. But he didn't.

In all his letters his signature looks still warm as if just having been written. Deep in his letters, in the middle of his sweeps, ups and downs, parallel strokes, the dazzling fireworks of gothic script, are crippled letters, like limp broken souls, unfinished looking, overlooked if one doesn't know what one is looking for. Letters that have a limp or a hump, letters that look like Carpenter Lohmann's naked legs: exposed and naked.

What did I do when he died? Did anyone hear him die? Are some of his bones left in the Ukrainian earth? Where did his hands that so often released the shutter of our Agfa to capture me, pride and apple of his eye, come to rest stripped by death and time?

His first card is dated August 9, 1943, written en route to the Ukraine. He had gotten past Lemberg, it took nine days. On August 10, he was in Zhitomir. His train was bombed by Russian planes, and guerrillas had blown up sections of the railroad. He was tired and exhausted, but didn't complain. His letters from this day on were sent by special SS-mail. He had joined the SS, and had his blood group tattooed in his armpit. He is waiting for mail from us. He's writing from headquarters in Zhitomir; he says he would like to have me with him for a few hours. In the same letter, he says that sixteen Russian guerrillas have been hung by the Germans in the town square. He uses the formal sentence: "Sixteen guerrillas have found their end by hanging, executed on the public square." It gives the impression that he thought it was a terrible but necessary action that could have been avoided if the guerrillas hadn't been so unreasonable.

Then there is a short letter just saying hello, and that he

is fine. He's supervising a munitions transport. He cuts down on eating and sends us a big can of meat. He's hoping his stay in Russia will end soon.

August 19. My father went swimming with his Ukrainian soldiers. It's very hot and dusty in Russia. He met an old friend on a little railway station by accident, and he is told the Americans had bombed Schweinfurt. He hopes Tante Anna is alive and well. He's afraid we might get bombed. September. He catches a cold he can't shake off. He received our package — cigarettes, matches, a flint for his lighter, and a cake — and he's glad. He is hunting guerrillas in the countryside, covering hundreds of miles each day. He supervises a wheat transport going to Germany. The nights are getting quite cold, not like the climate in Germany, he adds. A doctor suggests he be sent home right away because the winter would be dangerous to him. My father asks if I like school better now; he picks up some eggs in a village and makes himself an omelette. He feels lonely and would like to be with us, especially with me on Sunday mornings, with me running around in my pajamas. He constantly talks about me.

By the end of September, the German High Command had ordered all unnecessary things to be sent home; my father ships off some of his uniforms and asks my mother to have them cleaned. Time moves into October 1943. The German Army is retreating; my father is looking forward to his furlough in November, and he writes that he doesn't mind if my mother takes me out of religious instruction, since I seem to dislike it so much. He is constantly on patrol, trying to squash guerrilla activities. He goes to the movies, a comedy; he's asking us not to worry about him, he'll be alright, even if we shouldn't hear from him for some time. He is ordered to supervise 80,000 head of cattle going back to Germany. Most of the drive back is made on foot and only with friendly Ukrainian policemen. Zhitomir is falling to the Russians. He gets out just in time, and again he writes not to worry, everything will be all right. This is November 15, 1943, five days after my sixth birthday. I practiced my handwriting on the card; I copied the SS-insignia, SS-SS-SS-SS-Mail. I retraced my father's handwriting, his entire name, and on the back of the card, I wrote "father" "father" "father" — three times, one of the words I had learned to write. My father is in Bela Cerkov. And then comes his last letter, November 20, 1943, from Lysanka, about a hundred miles out of Kiev. He's worried about the cattle drive, there is not enough protection, not enough help, he isn't sure anymore of his Ukrainians, there are guerrillas all over the frozen woods. He ends with "Good Bye!" and "don't worry, kisses…"

Somewhere in the dark night of November 28/29, my father and his Ukrainians were ambushed by Russian guerrillas three kilometers west of Vladyslawczik. Silence falls forever. My father, the uncoded cipher sinks into the snows of Russia. The rest: kind letters from commanding officers, comrades, testimonials, my father's picture surrounded by laurels and the SS-insignia, in-the-name-of-the-Führer.

Nobody was present when life went out of him, no witnesses. He disappeared forever while I lay cuddled in my warm Franconian bed.

Although Russia had already swallowed my father, back in Franconia we put new film in our Agfa to take pictures of my father when he would come home for Christmas. My mother had also gotten a goose from a friendly farmer; we put her in a pen next to the raspberry patch. We also got five rabbits. Everybody was keeping rabbits to be eaten on feast day, because meat was hard to come by. My mother had hoarded food coupons and saved sugar for cakes, and Gertrude started to paint welcoming signs for my father. But our Agfa would never again capture my father in the filmy emulsion. No darkroom on earth could coax my father's image from any film; fate had dematerialized him. One day in December 1943 a police civil servant rang our bell to tell us so, after he asked my mother to sit down. We were in the living room, Frau Ritter from downstairs was just visiting. He said quietly that he was sorry to bring this news so close to Christmas, but my father had vanished on November 28; everything possible was being done to locate him, we could be sure of it.

Frau Ritter threw up her hands and wailed. She put her hand in front of her face, then moved them back up in the air. Oh God! Oh God! Frau Ritter moaned, the words went into each other without separation. My mother stared at her with amazement as if for a moment she wasn't sure if the man had spoken about my father or Herr Ritter; then she cried and called out my father's name: "Michael," she said, "Michael, why have you left us," as if it were his choosing.

I remember the civil servant and the two wailing women; I can't remember what I felt. Across from me was our big

Telefunken, my father's toy, now mine. A man in the dark said that missing in action didn't mean dead, there was still hope. "Ah," screamed Frau Ritter, "missing in action in Russia is worse than death!" She took her hands down and stared at the man as if she expected an answer. "Oh, poor man," she said, meaning my father, "why did it have to happen to you!?" She seemed to address my father; no answer came to her question. My father was already in the past tense.

My father the ghost, the once-body, my father the memory, the maker, who had injected his sperm into my mother to make me, had stepped across to the other side. He made me a half-orphan, my official designation on documents from now on, *"eine Halbwaise."* With the disappearance of my father, I began to suffer. It seemed as if there had been no suffering before. I suffered my state of being a half-orphan, a deprivation. But I not only suffered my own sufferings, I suffered my mother's too. She and I were one, both abandoned. Whoever attacked her attacked me. Whenever she cried, she cried my tears; we were both exposed to a hostile world, she said so. A woman could only try to "stand her man" as the German saying went, but it wasn't the same as being a man. I saw both of us on a gray plain in howling winds. We had lost our natural shelter. My mother said that there was no longer anyone to lean on. It happened to us both and sent pain into my extremities. We were both victims.

PART II

To Marilyn, my anima

❧25❧

S aint Michael was my father's patron saint. He had wings, a flaming sword and shield, and slew dragons. My father had a green motorcycle, black boots, and gendarme's gun. He was the archangel who killed my dragons until the dark slew him. I was left with St. Elisabeth of the Roses, twin flame to St. Michael: saint, wife, and widow, my mother with the triple crown. Her favorite mode of action: a kiss on my brow, "Ah, my poor little piglet." Soft moist lips, my St. Elisabeth mother.

By the fall of 1943, the dragons entered my territory from all directions. There were the monsters of the night: Lancasters, Wellingtons, Stirlings, Handley-Page Halifaxes that had been waiting for my father's departure. They flew deeper and deeper into the German Reich. We tried to ignore them but as the horror stories increased, we ran every time the sirens wailed. At night, they made my teeth chatter. The dark was coming at me.

Nights, when I was deep in comfortable sleep, the sirens rose to a high-pitched wail that rattled the windows. The sound penetrated my ears, shot down my spinal column and exited through my toes.

I dressed quickly in the cold room. Enemy planes on the chart over my bed were out there in the air. Olive green Lancasters with incendiary bombs. My bed looked warm and white under the soft light of the lamp. The folds threw cozy shadows, but I had to walk across the night garden. I knew that English pilots hung high up there in the night with oxygen masks on their faces. Massive hulks in black spaces were approaching.

We stumbled with our gas masks and emergency suitcases, I holding on to my mother. Our dark corridor had unusual shadows. Gertrude once put on woolen underpants for a sweater. She didn't notice it until people laughed in the shelter.

The other people in the dark hall sounded hollow and unearthly. The familiar had retreated. Territory I knew so well by day wore a different face.

The whole household crossed the garden to reach the Beyers' shelter. The night smelled unusual. Air rushed into my lungs as if it couldn't wait. The dark garden plunged toward me as if it wanted to tear me from my mother's hand and swallow me in a remote corner. Sometimes the sky was full of bright stars. My pear tree was a vague outline suspended in the night. During a bright moon, a voice would always say, "That's perfect night-bombing weather...!" The moon was dangerous.

The Beyers stood at the door of their shelter. Inside it was warm. People talked about lost sleep and cursed the Allies. Somewhere a faucet was dripping. People fell asleep. I rested my head against my mother, or curled up on the pillow she had brought. I wanted to sleep but couldn't because of the strangers in the room and glaring light from the naked bulb. Herr Beyer always yawned and rubbed his mouth afterwards as if he had to get his mouth ready for the next yawn. I saw a dazed spider on the ceiling and wondered if the light kept him awake too.

All-clear signal. The siren slowly died while we crossed the garden on the way back to my white bed. The low expiring blast sounded like the moaning of an animal, an unknown creature in the dark curling up to sleep again. The night tempted me to stay as I hurried to get home.

Not only the RAF let loose dark dragons. We had our

own family monster, Aunt Augusta, pronounced with a strong explosive emphasis on the second syllable of her name and she was proud of it.

During the warm August nights of 1943 the English flew over Hamburg where my aunt lived and incinerated it. Everything she owned went up in flames and she escaped, so she said, with her naked life and her emergency suitcase. With it she outran the firestorm that burned up thousands of people. She came to calm Franconia to stay with us.

Aunt Augusta was nine years older than my mother and took over our fatherless household, especially me, who she said, was too soft and too southern. I needed some northern drive. I was small and malleable and if she didn't do something soon, I'd turn into a southern weakling. I was petrified.

I stood in front of Aunt Augusta who wagged a finger in front of my eyes and told me she had two sons who had to go to bed at eight in the summer and at seven during winter. I was going to do the same. My mother didn't say a thing. Discipline was good for little boys!

She came to my bed every morning and clapped her hands. "Time to rise," she said, pulling me out of bed. She marched me to the kitchen and filled a basin with ice-cold water, took out our natural sponge, and stripped off my pajamas. She washed my chest with the cold water. "That will make a real man out of you," she said breathlessly, because the rubbing had taken her breath away. "I did it every day to my sons and they are fine German soldiers today, one in Denmark, the other in Romania."

I shivered, tears in my eyes, rage in my heart. Aunt Augusta held me down with an iron grip, the sponge crushed my eyeballs and my eardrums as she looked for dirt in every corner of my head.

I turned on our *Telefunken* to hear if the RAF was still bombing Hamburg, because my mother had said that Aunt Augusta would go back as soon as things quieted down. But the Allies were still active all over northern Germany and Aunt Augusta stayed on.

She was all movement and power. There was no peace in her, she was a crusader and went after things; there was no hiding from her. When she heard about my impersonations of Zarah Leander, she looked at me and said, "Hmm." After that she used more cold water in the mornings and scrubbed my soul harder. She got after Gertrude for being lazy and hysterical. But Gertrude just stomped her feet and screamed, "I won't do it," and Aunt Augusta retreated. I didn't dare follow suit. I was the dragon's victim of her stringent preparations for my future life. She told me indirectly that I had to be corrected — corrections terrified me. To be in need of corrections meant one was imperfect. My mother thought I was perfect, but she was like a warm sputtering flame compared to the blaze of her sister.

I had strange dreams: it was night and I entered our garden wearing one of my mother's wartime sweaters knitted from remnants, full of dropped stitches. I came to the gate between our garden and the Beyers'. An identical other me stood on the other side. He smiled seductively. We shook hands. I ran upstairs to wash my hands, because the other me had been poisonous. In the sink boiled a cup of fire; the fire flared up in an explosion that blew me through the air down to the Landwehrplatz. I stood on the oval of the park and looked at a red-orange full moon that started spinning faster and faster until I was dizzy and started to spin too. Aunt Augusta woke me up at that point to say that it was seven in the morning and time for the icy sponge.

26

My existence had become perilous. Ploesti was still smoking. During the day, Schweinfurt was bombed by great fleets of B-17s. At night, the RAF hung in the dark skies, and at home Aunt Augusta slammed her presence into every corner of the gendarmerie. Only four years before, Germany had destroyed Poland, now the Germans were retreating from Russia. And I had to go to school.

I didn't want to. I had learned to read by myself. I was able to decode as much as I needed: the black and white ciphers of Zarah and the mystic combinations of planes and pilots! I could tell anyone who wanted to know that one of the top German aces had shot down 301 enemy planes. Erich Hartmann, as many as 352. He flew a Messerschmidt Bf-109G. Galland on the other hand preferred a Bf-109F. I combined Messerschmidt and Leander. I knew the national anthem. I could spell Hitler, Göring, and Goebbels. I grasped the world in headlines. But in spite of everything, they told me that September 1, 1943, would be my entry into the real world. I hesitated and nearly convinced my mother to postpone my appearance on the large plane of things for another year because I was only five and a half. But Aunt Augusta saw to it that I went. She took me to school herself.

Because of her I remember so much about my first day at school. All the mothers went with their children except mine. She had yielded me to Aunt Augusta, therefore to the world.

Summer was nearly over. September had wobbly and shifting warm days, sun-gray in texture, hazy clouds. The linden trees had peaked. Their green was going downhill

137

when Aunt Augusta brought me to school: the Roman Catholic Elementary School for Boys at the end of the Schrannenstrasse. I had Gertrude's old leather satchel strapped to my back, pre-war quality, eternal, they all said. Waxed and polished, made from Franconian cows. I had a new wooden box with a removable top. Inside: pencils and slate stylos for writing on the small slate blackboards we all possessed. A sponge in a green box to wipe the slate clean, eraser, and pencil sharpener.

We assembled in the courtyard and sang the national anthem under a limp September swastika next to the tall chestnut trees of the St. Johannis Kirche, late Renaissance. Dark green trees with sun spots coming through. We raised our hands: *Heil Hitler!* Then we went inside. Hard smell of oiled floors and sweating children. For me it was an aggressive alien odor.

Frau Baumann was my first teacher. She had black braids wrapped around her head and wore the party button over her heart. She ordered the parents to the back of the room, and sorted us out according to height. The mothers didn't say a word, which made a deep impression on us. Even parents were helpless before Frau Baumann. She ruled unopposed, especially over us, the fatherless. We sat down according to height. Frau Baumann had judged and ranked us already. I became aware there was a hierarchy, and I was about in the center of it.

Frau Baumann stood erect in front of us. In the corner to her left was a large cane. Behind her on the wall, Hitler: sepia-red, looking into the easterly direction. He had better things to do than to watch us.

Frau Baumann squeezed her arms tightly against her body. Her hands made fists. Erect and proper, no mysteries, no secrets. She said she was a just teacher to all children, no matter where they came from. She didn't look at anybody, she looked at the back wall above the heads of our mothers. When she finally looked into our eyes, we were grateful to her. Frau Baumann was a clear, rapid brook that couldn't be opposed. I would have to rush along with it. I was prepared to obey. I tried to tell her so with my eyes, but deep down I was lying. After her speech, she raised her hand and said firmly: *"Heil Hitler!"* Everybody in the room quickly repeated it after her. Everything was as irrefutable as the Reich, which we had officially entered. It expected contributions from us, Frau Baumann said. I sat stiffly on my bench.

When Frau Baumann walked into class for the first time she carried an alarm clock in her hands. Incorruptible time-piece. It fixed her forever in my mind. The clock ticked within its white and chrome cylinder with its back to us. Only Frau Baumann knew what time it was — she controlled time. When she was quiet, her clock spoke for her; and we listened to the dripping minutes and seconds, fast, slow, escaping into the void around us, and waited until the clock's mistress told us the hour had struck. Frau Baumann's clock followed me home and ticked away across weekends reminding me that Monday would be coming. It ticked as the symbol of events to come, inescapable events.

On that first day in school, Tante Augusta did a terrible thing. Toward the end of our first meeting, Frau Baumann asked how many children could already read and write. I proudly stuck up my hand, ready to recite movie stars and Luftwaffe aces as well as all the capitals of the world we had conquered. Frau Baumann nodded, smiled, and asked if any of the children could do something special. There was a long silence, the puzzled mothers were tying to remember. It was then the horror stuck right into the public silence. Aunt Augusta pointed to me and said in her loud northern accent that made everyone pull back with respect that her nephew could do Zarah Leander. My blood rushed down through my feet and out into the cracks of the oiled floors. My ears burned like furnaces. The word Zarah made me faint. I stood naked in front of Frau Baumann, my classmates and their mothers. Their eyes saw every little detail. My blood rushed back up through the floors and shot into my head. My insides burst out: my heart and liver, my spleen, lungs, testicles and intestines were hanging from a clothesline strung across the room of strangers. Aunt Augusta had pinned them up herself. My lips moved by themselves and said, "I've forgotten."

27

My mother was the only screen between me and the world, but she couldn't catch all the insidious drafts that swept Franconia. Her kiss and "Ah, my little sausage!" wasn't enough. My father's winged sword was missing. The curtain had gone up and I felt alone on the stage. I was attacked by illnesses, the slightest chill gave me a fever. I loved and dreaded illness: my gaze wandered sluggishly up the wall over the blue madonna in our bedroom. Her eyes were more contorted than usual. Noise from outside sounded drowsy and hollow. I felt nauseated and couldn't find the right side to lie on, days went on without me. I escaped Frau Baumann's clock. I made my own time: wobbly, sluggish measured by thermometers and my mother's cold wrists. Time ached in the eyeballs as it moved across the day.

I was allowed to look at my father's deluxe World War I books. *The Air War over Flanders*. A German plane shooting down an English one. The enemy's insignias looked like evil, poisonous eyes. They stared right at me. I put the book down and picked it up again. Precise details: types of planes, dates, places, the Cathedral of Rheims. I knew its ruins by heart. An old woman was standing in front of it with a push-cart. I became involved in aerial dogfights. I wondered what happened to crashed aviators, how they would escape through enemy territory. Exhausted, I put the book down. World War I took place while I was sick. It was an encapsulated war that occurred in my feverish skull. My hot bed exhaled it, skinny planes flew through sluggish air over the dark trenches in my sheets.

I had the measles. Aunt Anna was visiting and brought me pears. My hearing went away and came back. While I had a temperature of 102, the sirens went off, full alarm. My mother raised her hands in front of her mouth and said: "Holy Mary! What are we going to do with Winfried?" Sirens outside came from another dimension, and Aunt Anna said, "Let's put him into the laundry basket."

It was a wicker basket, the color of light straw. I was wrapped in a blanket, a pillow under my head and a feather bed on top. Two gendarmes carried me to the Beyers'.

I floated from the intimate fever of my bed into the outside world. The handles creaked at every step, past Hitler and Göring, still in their frames in spite of my illness. They moved by in a dreamlike trance. I was exhaled into the garden, the cold air went into my lungs. In the shelter was the usual soft, warm bubbling porridge of voices, strangers from the street: they parted before me and the gendarmes. I, my father's son, the measles case. I felt I had been caught in an

141

indecent act, exposed in my sick bed to the healthy world. With the faint sound of planes overhead, everybody looked to the ceiling as if the answer was written there.

Then I caught scarlet fever. It hatched in our bedroom now deserted by my father. It was winter. They put me into the warm living room where I watched the spidery design of the wallpaper: chrysanthemums, tarantulas, snowflakes, ice flowers, cities, and giraffes until I was dizzy.

In the evening, my mother went into her lullaby pose and sang *"Guten Abend, Gute nacht, mit Rosen bedacht,"* or *"Die ersten Sternlein prangen am grossen Himmelszelt."* Whenever she came to the line, *"Schlupf unter die Deck…"* of the first song, I felt like passing away into wonderful sleep. The word *"schlupf"* radiated comfortable oblivion. White clean sheets, soft light — my mother had put a scarf over the lamp, good night, mellow dark. My mother's lips felt cool just before sleep.

28

C ures were slipped into the stupor of illness through teas, sweating cures, and letting-nature-take-its-course. I inhaled and drank teas: linden, chamomile, wormwood, lilac, and red rose. Nature took it from there, as if she were warmed up by a good sweat.

I was rolled in wet, hot sheets. They felt comfortable like a hot bath, steam rising from my body, feather beds piled on top of me. Sweating was a pleasurable pain. It ran down my body, behind my ears, between my legs. Big drops tickled my groin, dripped on my scrotum, which first contracted then slackened, finally the sweat ran down my rear end. I was like the murky water of Moon Lake across the river where we went swimming in the summer. I floated deeper and deeper into the steaming bed space. I was in a hot tunnel with health at the other end. The light. Time tickled away in sweat balls, I pushed myself to endure one more minute, then another, and another. I discharged impurities, salty, bitter drops my body didn't want. I relished the sensation. The drops had faces, the space around me contracted...they unrolled me like a steaming sausage, and the room was flooded with light. I was weak but getting better.

꧁29꧂

My mother said the world must go on, that she had to be brave and live for her children. That's what my father would have wanted. She wiped her eyes, her mouth puckered, and then she became brave. I looked to the floor or past her into a corner. It was a ritual. Everybody gave her sympathy by nodding and looking grave. Some of her women friends cried a little. Then they wound up talking about food. My mother still had glittering tears in her eyes. Although the tears belonged to my father, my mother's eyes already belonged to somewhere else. The crisis had passed. She wiped the last moisture out of her eyes, and I watched it evaporate on the skin of her fingers. Sometimes she even laughed while doing it.

My mother wasn't the only one who cried. Holding her hand, I entered other women's living rooms, polished and

waxed like tombs, the curtains drawn. Somebody's son or husband had been killed and my mother went to console them as they consoled her. "I know how it feels..." my mother said and put on her good coat from before the war. After I shook hands with the women and made a little gentleman's bow, I was deposited on a hard chair and left to myself. I watched the women.

They all cried the same basic way with small personal variations: quiet tears fell from red eyes, the mouth quivered, they wiped their eyes with fingers while making fluttery hopeless gestures afterwards as if they wanted to fling the tears away. They deposited their tears with short moist explosions through their noses into tiny handkerchiefs, which they stuck into their sleeves only to retrieve them again and start all over. By the end of the visit the handkerchiefs were soaked through and the women's noses were red and pointed, as if the constant use of the handkerchief had made them longer.

The women's motions had become habit, their bodies reacted automatically. They went through gestures of a creeping national epidemic: quiet grief, pinched look in black clothes. My mother didn't wear black because her husband was only missing-in-action. She was in the "*Vermisst*-category" and felt most comfortable with women in the same group: they had a glimmer of hope. The women whose husbands had been killed were above them in terms of grief. I sat and watched women in grief: sad beings who kept saying: "*Ja, Ja,*" with a perplexed look, the second "*ja*" hardly audible, a shadow of breath colored by vaporous tears, usually repeated at the door when we left.

Everybody turned around once more to look silently at an enlarged photograph of the mourned man placed in a conspicuous spot of the room and draped in black crepe. The faces of the men gave no indication that they knew what grief they had caused. Usually the stiff epaulettes of their uniforms lifted their faces upwards into rigid smiles that reached beyond death. But as this went on, I saw so many photographs of fallen soldiers that I thought I could see in a photograph if the person was dead or alive. Many of the photographs had been primitively retouched and gave the faces unnaturally smooth, pale complexions without lines and wrinkles, reminding me of the mask-like faces that Lieutenant Nüsslein and Herr Kolb had shown in their coffins. I didn't know anything about retouching and came to believe that I could see death in these faces. I instinctively avoided those photographs, because I felt an icy pull coming form them. Their proper uniforms were a dangerous illusion; they held decay and death and mystery together and gave it the semblance of life.

▧30▧

I accepted the fact I now lived in a world of women. They accomplished everything, although ultimate authority came from men. As more and more men went off to war, women took their places. All the women said the same thing: *"Wer hätte das gedacht..."* "Who would have thought that it would come to this?" They went on to say it couldn't be helped, they had to suffer, but they expected to surrender their present roles which they had usurped from men at sometime in the future, when peace would restore the old world. I was living in a temporary world, the war-world in which old rules no longer applied. Children were to be pitied because they had to endure war. "Why did we bring children into the world?" they said shaking their heads. We were poor worms, *Würmchen.* I felt a soft glow from all the sympathy but didn't understand much else because war was all I could remember.

Christmas 1943 was my first fatherless Christmas. It lacked the lights my father used to turn on. I came down with rheumatism in my left leg, followed by a minor case of rickets. My ankles and wrists grew thin, my chest caved in. I got pampered. I even got real milk, not the thin blue skim milk Frau Lachmann sold from her cans. Because of me we even got additional supplies of coal, which we burned in the living room where I looked at World War I again, and wondered where the old woman in black with the pushcart was now.

As 1943 declined, so did German strength. The Allies increased their activities. At a series of conferences in far-flung places that we found in my sister's atlas, they met to decide on my fate. Cairo, Casablanca, Teheran, Aunt Anna said, were the cause for my rickets! Her house had been blown up by the Americans in Schweinfurt. She brought a new game with her, inspired by the Allied meeting.

In the evening, as soon as the blackout curtains were drawn, we sat around the table and played blowing-up-the-Allies. All we needed were matches and a clothespin.

Aunt Anna emptied the matches on the table, snipped off one of the match tops and stuck the explosive head in the prongs of the open clothespin. It looked like an alligator whose mouth was forcefully opened. Then she put the empty lower half of the matchbox on the top of the clothespin, which represented a hotel in Teheran. She did all the voices herself: a knock, the hotel owner answered, and Stalin asked for a room. Stalin was a matchstick Aunt Anna put to bed in the hotel. Then Roosevelt came and was put in the same bed. Finally Churchill. Then Hitler asked for a bed. He was invited to join the others but refused. He lit the match between the clothespin and with a hissing explosion the hotel blew sky high. Everybody applauded and Aunt Anna said that she would wring Churchill's neck personally if she had the chance. He was behind everything. He was the cause of suffering and the terrible bombings. Churchill was a gangster of the worst kind, a killer of innocent children.

I believed Aunt Anna and I loved fires. I enjoyed lighting matches. The fat hiss of the igniting match head gave me thorough satisfaction.

Watching a match ignite, the smell of sulfur and a succession of colors gave release to some hidden part of me. I wasn't allowed to play with matches until Aunt Anna's game came along. Now I could play blowing up the enemy to my heart's content. Fire had become patriotic and for several days I played Teheran until I had blown up the entire city.

During cold winter afternoons, my aunt and mother sat in the warm kitchen and talked about the past over ersatz coffee and war cake. I sat with them, secure. Everyday life shut out everything else. I didn't want to be anywhere else. Women ruled quietly from the inside. It was idyllic in our big kitchen with cake, coffee, and talk of the past. Memories were like strolling through dried flower forest, shadows in long black skirts, midwives everywhere. The sun and moon were shining down on straw flowers.

I knew the stories by heart. There was Aunt Anna who had measles. She nearly went blind. Grandmother got a retired midwife who put fresh cheese on her eyes. It *had* to be cheese with whey to draw out the blindness. My mother said it was the soul of fermented cheese that did it! Aunt Augusta, when young, had a swollen neck. Nothing helped. Grandmother sent her to an 80-year-old midwife. She took Aunt Augusta up a mountain on the night of a full moon. She prayed over my aunt's neck, spoke incantations. They repeated this every night until the moon waned. So did my aunt's swollen neck. My mother shook her head slowly, raised her shoulders, and made a doubtful face. "I don't know," she said, "but it worked!" And the third story, the most unusual: my mother had an infected finger. The doctor wanted to lance it, but she ran off. Grandmother sent her to an old wise woman called the baroness. The old woman told her what to do. Here my mother always put her hands in front of her face and giggled. She said that she wasn't sure if could go on with the story, but she always did. The next time she had a bowel movement, she caught some of the warm stool in a bandage, and wrapped it around the finger. It remained on the finger the whole night. It pulled and tugged but by the net morning the infection had risen to the surface and could be drained.

The woman's cures were odorous romances, self-contained idylls, each with its own particular perfume. Whenever a child had whooping cough the child was brought into the warm stables where the animals' exhalations cured the cough. Pungent straw whose basic colors were brown and yellow. When someone suffered from rheumatism her or she stuck their hands or arms into a huge ant heap in the forest. The ants' poison cured rheumatism. Red-brown, moving and teeming, and the basic smell was thin black acid. Or, a bottle half-filled with *spiritus* was stuck overnight into the ant heap; the ants crawled in and drowned. The enriched alcohol was rubbed on the rheumatic limbs. It smelled like plum schnapps plus ants' legs. If people had circulatory problems they had to walk barefoot through wet meadows before the sun rose. Summer hay, wet and heavy fragrance, clover; smell of a wet sun. While I listened I watched the white cameo brooches on the women's breasts. They moved up and down between the cleavage, just below the spot where some of the white soft flesh was visible in the neckline. The stories fused with the smell of cologne 4711; no woman existed without it.

Their past filled my mind like comforting, fragrant smoke. I relived what they had left behind so long ago yet still nourished and kept alive. Through their tones of voice, I heard that a baroness was far above a greengrocer's daughter. The baroness took on hues of silky colors moving majestically through the past of Münnerstadt, dispensing health and revealing secrets that my mother eagerly absorbed and transmitted to her son. I lived my mother's past. She was so much happier then. For example, the time she caught frogs in the pond and let them loose at the dance. She was the princess! Men courted her! She turned them away, many a good match, she said smiling. She played practical jokes all day, and a good time it was, picking apples and pears. She flirted with seminary students who loitered on the square, and took boat rides up the little river in Bad Kissingen on hot shady afternoons in white gauze dresses. She stepped off the boat for lemonade, and I forgot I wasn't my mother.

As the year 1944 went on, my father receded and women took over everything. I imitated more and more my mother's method of reaction: absorption rather than attack. In school one day Frau Baumann hit me full force across the face, because I had done what she had said not to do — start an essay in the same line as the title. I flew off the podium and stumbled to regain my equilibrium. Though fighting tears of rage and hurt, I did nothing. I said nothing. I waited for times to improve, my mother's favorite approach.

During those winter conversations around the kitchen table with my mother, my aunts and her friends, I — by re-living my mother's past — slipped clandestinely back into her vagina, past what Germans call the "mother's mouth," into her womb, and from there I invaded all of her body where I had been all along while she was living what was now the "past." I was more a product of my mother than my father. His sperm had coaxed me out. It was natural that my ties to my mother-past were stronger than those to my father. After all, his part of me had been distilled like spirits from his body and expelled by him into my mother who took in the home-less sperm-me, and engulfed me with my egg-self, poured herself over me protectively, while I woke up and started to imbibe her juices, making her big like the cows in Kuhn's stables that bulged with health. I was my mother, slightly rearranged by my father's aggressive sperm.

ৠ31ৱ

At the time I entered school, Italy betrayed Germany, but daring German paratroopers rescued Mussolini and put matters right. It was clear we couldn't trust the south. Germany was open on all sides now, and by spring 1944, Russia reached the frontiers of Romania.

In Kitzingen, the linden trees and the chestnuts unfurled their leaves on schedule as if nothing was happening, although the Landwehrplatz had seen great changes. The Röhmers' apartment had been taken over by a family called Riedel. They were below us in rank and not as clean as the Röhmers had been. They had three daughters, Anneliese, Margarete and Hildegard, all older than me, and not right for afternoon tea in the tree house, since they didn't have any tea services. Their hair looked unwashed. They didn't play the piano. They were very Roman Catholic.

But a far more important event had just taken place: a group of Russian prisoners had moved into town. The men lived in the synagogue, women and children in the Jewish school.

They were foreigners and enemies. We were not supposed to speak with them, we couldn't speak their language anyway. They came from eternal snows. They had killed my father. Russians had disease and lice. Outcasts, slaves.

The deck was stacked against the Russians.

I stood next to Herr Heim's carpenter shop and watched the gutted synagogue where the Russians lived. I pretended I was waiting for friends to play with, but my eyes were turned to the doors where the Russians came and went supervised by German guards. Their heads were shaved; they smelled of disinfectant. They carried their smell with them wherever they went, identifying them as disreputable and illegal.

I was attracted by the alien territory the Russians created in our midst. The men's bodies radiated otherwise. I was drawn to them in the same way rivers must follow the sea. Maybe some of my suspect ancestors woke from their sleep in my genes. I longed to enter the synagogue, but didn't dare.

Passion creates opportunities, which look like chance. About the same time the allies landed in Normandy, catching us by surprise, I watched a summer downpour from the Beyers' door. Across from me under the entrance of the Jewish School stood a little Russian boy my age doing the same. He had a shaved head. When the sun came out and the asphalt steamed, he took off his shoes and ran through the puddles. I took off my shoes and followed him down the Glauberstrasse.

On the large scale of events, our armies were fighting the Allies on the beaches of Normandy: in the circumference of my own plain, I was walking hand in hand, Russian-style, with a small Russian along the riverbanks. We became inseparable, united by a summery downpour. He put his arm around my neck and took me inside the synagogue to visit his father who smelled of delousing powder and stirred a huge pot that contained a slimy bubbling mass: their lunch. The stovepipe went through one of the star-shaped windows of the synagogue. His father looked at me with apprehension, since Germans were not allowed inside the synagogue.

Somebody talked to my mother about her son: I was seen all the time with a little Russian. What could I possibly learn from a Russian? It wasn't correct, I should stick to my German friends. My mother said we were too young to understand politics, and I continued my questionable friendship.

All things Russian had been reduced to a small scale in my friend. He was compact and much stronger than me. He was direct, knew what he wanted and did it. The Russian led, I followed. As soon as I could in the morning, I ran across the street where he waited for me under the door of the abandoned Jewish School. Irmtraud was a thousand miles away in my mind; she would never have condoned the little Russian as her rival. I smuggled him into our garden, up into the tree house. His shaved head gave him away as a Russian and the gendarmes stared at him from the office windows. But they said nothing because I was still my father's son, though my father had vanished in my friend's homeland. They mocked him by pinching their noses in his direction to indicate that all Russians stank. I inhaled the Russian smell that emanated from all parts of his body and stuck in clothes much too small for him. When we knelt together on the ground, I drew close to him as if I could absorb him through my nose and eyes. I watched his hands and arms move — they were moved by a center I wanted to know. I wanted an act of magic to occur: my clothes would be thrown off and I would be transported into his and inhabit them with him. We would be one. But the German Reich had no tolerance for my private dreams. The Russians suddenly disappeared into night and fog. I was stunned by their absence. The doors were wide open and the smell of disinfectant was the only sign left. I entered the school and walked through the empty rooms.

§32§

I was the best reader and writer in class and was moved into the second class halfway through the first. Aunt Anna always said that I knew too much for my age and that wasn't good. "Mind my words!" she said, "it's not natural." She shook her head as if she wanted to shake it out of her mind. During one of her visits, I stuck a long rusty needle in her bed, the point facing upwards, and carefully concealed it with the blanket. It stuck in her thigh. She let out a high-pitched squeal and everybody ran to her room. I stayed behind in my bed. I could see them in the hall, my aunt holding the needle upward for everyone to see. "Only Winfried could have done this," she said, pointing in my direction. "He has seen too many films!"

By June 20, 1944, I could read headlines fluently. Traitors had tried to assassinate the Führer. We stood around the Linden Square and looked at photographs in the papers. Hitler was showing Mussolini the destroyed room where the bomb had gone off. Hitler looked gray and weak.

Everybody talked about the terrible plot, the traitors. The Riedel children said all the traitors would be hanged and they deserved it. My mother read the court proceedings to me.

On the photograph a traitor stood under a swastika flanked by policemen. My mother dramatized the dialogue. The president of the court asked the traitor with what specific animal he identified himself. The traitor said: "With the ass." The judge thundered: "No! My dear Sir, you are a *Schweinehund!*" which echoed back from the walls and bounced in front of my eyes. "Poor people," my mother said, " but why did they have to do things like that?" The word "dog-of-a-swine" uttered by a judge produced effects. It was the ultimate condemnation of a terrible crime beyond my understanding, treason. My mother cut out the entire trial and saved it as historical memorabilia.

The headlines that cluttered the Linden Square on discarded newspapers made us suspect that tremendous things were going on in the distance. But after a few days everything returned to normal and the traitors were executed. My sister Ilse joined the Party, and my mother had to join the national war effort. Two nights a week she had to go to a local factory where she closed the lids on cartons containing artificial honey. Ilse wore the party button and went off the Hammelburg with the *Arbeitisdienst* where she had to take care of an old lady. Gertrude, next in line for the BDM, said that she would never join. Soon I would be ready for the Hitler Youth and a brown uniform. I would be a skinny Hitler youth, however; bad food and midnight trips to air raid shelters showed up on the Agfa records. I show a worn smile to the camera.

• • •

Neither the RAF nor the USAAF had dropped anything on Kitzingen yet, but one day the sirens went off exactly at noon, B-24s appeared out of the blue and tried to hit the railway bridge in the south of town. All the bombs missed, sounding like distant thunder. Everything was over quickly and we emerged form the Beyers' shelter. We had been warned, the enemy hadn't forgotten us.

Soon afterwards the anti-aircraft guns went off at night. From the kitchen window we watched tracer bullets flying into the sky like celestial fireworks. Instead of running to the shelter we were hypnotized by the spectacle. We heard planes overhead and suddenly colored flares floated from the skies over Kitzingen. The apple gendarme screamed from downstairs that this was it; we were going to burn tonight. The whole house ran to the shelter; the Riedels screamed and prayed. We all knew that the flares, nicknamed Christmas trees, were always dropped by lead planes to mark the target for the following bomber fleets. We sat on the pre-war orange crates and waited with pounding hearts for the sound of the monster Lancasters that had killed 50,000 in Hamburg; the fire had consumed all the oxygen and people suffocated in the streets and cellars. Aunt Augusta had vividly described people in flames running through the streets and jumping into the harbor to douse the burning phosphor. My heart stopped at the faintest sound. What did the English want in Kitzingen? The RAF didn't come that night. The apple gendarme explained the bombers didn't see the flares and missed the target. The Riedels said a loud prayer of thanks before we went upstairs.

▧33▧

I had started to chew and suck the leather straps of my school satchel. My mother was embarrassed about it. The straps looked pockmarked and sapped by my saliva. I couldn't help it. I couldn't resist my oral craving. On the way to school, waiting to cross a street, I chewed with passion. I tried to hide it; finally I wasn't even aware that I chewed in public. The straps were always there, never diminished. I simply reshaped them. Only in Frau Baumann's presence did I resist; but I could feel the straps tempting me insidiously. Firm, yet pliable, stringent in taste, the chemistry of spit and old leather had become addictive. I sucked and chewed and rolled them with my tongue. I wanted to chew out the very soul of the leather. My mother sensed there was an underlying reason for my chewing passion, but mainly treated it as a destructive streak in me that sought to destroy a perfectly good pre-war satchel impossible to replace. But I was sucking on something more profound.

I also had another habit, which worried my mother. I looked like an idiot doing it, she said. I ran the fingernails of my right hand over my earlobes, particularly when they were cold. Something urged me to absorb the coolness of my earlobes with my fingernails.

At this time Germany began to fire its secret weapon, the V-1 rocket, against England. Between June 13 and September 14, 1944, we sent 8,600 to the enemy. We all had *Vergeltungsfieber* (revenge fever) and followed daily news bulletins to learn how many we had launched. I wanted to know what the English did when the rockets hit London; I was interested in the immediate effect, but I got evasive answers. Nobody had pictures of what the bombs actually did, except that they caused "unchecked terror and destruction" as the radio announced in a loud, strident voice. On the Landwehrplatz, we interrupted our games and ran home at news-time to get the latest and then returned re-telling each other the V-1 news. In our games, we became V-1s and hurled ourselves against the enemy.

Already during my Irmtraud era we had played war games. We were Ju-87s and He-111s sitting in the airy pear tree as we bombed the cabbages and lettuce below. Each cabbage was an enemy capital; London was the biggest cabbage. We bombed them with twigs and little rocks, and reported damage in the manner of the *Deutschlandssender*. Afterward, we studied the damage through binoculars the way Hitler had looked at burning Warsaw. Or I bombarded Irmtraud as she approached with her tea set and said she was an enemy ship and I a Focke-Wulf 200 Condor with a range of over 2,000 miles.

We had airplanes and bombs circling in our brains; the Allies' bombing of Germany reached all-time highs in the summer of 1944. Every time our *Telefunken* transmitted news, it announced the cities-bombed-of-the-day. When Germany launched the first V-2s we got delirious. We became ballistic missiles that struck from the sky and turned London into an inferno.

My friend Rolfi said that we were working on a rocket that would reach New York. New York was so far away that it was nearly untrue. We all knew London as if it was in our backyard. But New York was behind a large ocean. We knew that it had skyscrapers that would crumble under our rockets. We were also producing planes that could fly to America and back. We had secret weapons everywhere. Rolfi said all we had to do was trust the government; they knew what they were doing. Gertrude said the same. A year later, when the Americans were already in Biebelried, she still claimed our secret weapons would turn them away.

We became countries; we declared war against each other; we tried to follow the rules of the big world. It was called "war." It became the Linden Square's favorite game, obliterating all other games.

We drew a circle in the earth of the Linden Square and divided it like a pie. Each one of us got a slice, we all were different countries. And then we went to war; we had war fever. Someone stood in the middle of the pie and announced, "I declare war on..." and then named one of the countries of the pie. This country had to rush quickly as possible to the center and shout "stop," while the others tried to escape as fast as possible from the pie. Whoever was in the middle had five large steps to reach someone. If he did, he could take a slice of his country away and add it to his. We fought furiously to make our slices bigger and bigger. It was all in the speed, like our Blitzkrieg in Poland. Slow people like

Anneliese Spatz, who had a little mustache on her upper lip and hair on her legs, always lost everything. She tried to defend her country, but it was divided up among the fast ones without mercy. War was war; borders had to be extended; that was simply in the nature of things.

ᔕ34ᔓ

The war made us glow like engine exhaust of the fast FW190 - power, speed, and destruction. To strike from the sky in a cataclysm of fire and explosions was a psychic necessity. Our imagination foreshortened space and time: we reconquered Russia in a matter of minutes we covered her vast expanses the circumference of the Linden Square was the entire world accessible with our wings: we became He-177 Greifs and mythical Ju-290s. When the fabulous Me-Komet appeared in the German skies, we launched the jet era on Linden Square. The Komet was rocket-propelled and flew faster than anything else in the world. Our passion for speed reached frenzy.

The summer of 1944 was a miracle of technology. Komets, V-1s, V-2s. When the radio announced that 200 German bombers had launched a surprise attack on fleets of American B-17s and Mustangs stationed on Russian airfields, we became euphoric. Our arms grew into airplane wings, we became two- engine or four-engine bombers. We obliterated the RAF and USAAF together.

Power was enclosed in mystic combinations of letters and numbers: Me-163, He-178, V-1, V-2, He-177, Ju-290. Each combination radiated its own formula of destruction; each unit was a potential fireball. The Me-163s and V-2s hurled through space generating their own combinations of sound and motion. The He-177 was lighter and less deadly than the He-178. The Me-163 was bright and lurked in the day; the Ju-290 hung in the night; it droned in high darkness.

But the Me-163s and V-2s were also magic ciphers against our own terror inspired by the fleets of Allied bombers that circled incessantly over Germany. We were always on the edge of being their target; they could appear any time and blot out the sun over Kitzingen. In the summer of 1944, we lapsed into another game with the energy of desperation; we became engineers of shelters and bunkers.

In our garden, next to the raspberry bushes where we now had some ducks to supply us with meat, we dug holes in the murky mud left behind by the ducks. We reinforced holes with twigs and rocks. We built ceilings with wet mud and waited until everything had dried. Then we bombed our own creations to see how much they could take.

I became a specialist in underground bunkers; they promised the greatest security. I created a new method: a combination of twigs and heavy mud, letting it dry and applying new layers. I wanted ultimate safety. On top of the mud came dry twigs inside in upright positions: men, women, and children. Then we bombed with rockets and dive-bombers. I worried about the occupants inside my bunkers. Would they survive? I tried to imagine what it felt like to be inside: cool darkness with destruction from above. I imbued them with soul and emotion. When the ceiling cracked under the bombardment we had launched, my heart pounded and I examined the damage afterward, trying to establish how many twigs had died or survived. I placed myself in the darkest and securest corners; I always survived. I became both the bomber and the bombed.

From bunkers, we progressed to dams we filled with duck water. We built towns and cities below, then we bombed, using the earthquake bombs the Allies had sent against German dams: 22,000-pound bombs that shook the earth as we watched floods unleashed into our towns. Afterward: expert opinions, cold-blooded analysis of damage and effectiveness of methods of bombing. The universe was a gigantic time bomb waiting to go off. Our games were a miniature version. We set off small explosions within the gigantic one. Everything was a matter of refining concentrated explosive force. We tried to outdo each other in bomb tonnage and in protection against it. Our games became more and more elaborate. We smuggled in plywood panels for ceilings, which was against our own rule which said that building materials had to come from the garden. We wanted our creations to survive and others to be destroyed. Toward the end of the day, we fell into uncontrolled frenzy and discarded all rules; we used building blocks as bombs, bombed everything and everybody, even our own creations. In order to make our work look more realistic, we became more and more resourceful. We stole chunks of poisonous-smelling carbide from the technical emergency service and stuck it into the bunkers and factories we had built. We added water: foam, explosions, white gases, and harsh chemical smells rose into the air: the English Midlands, the Rührgebiet was burning in the duck corner of our garden. With final suicide attacks, we turned designs into reeling chaos. Exhausted, we stared at the apocalypse. I went back up to our apartment and surprised my mother because I was as clean as I had been in the morning, and didn't have a single hair out of place.

The words *"Polen"* and *"Russen"* were on the same level: voices went down a notch or two when they were pronounced. Both were Slavs, *Slawen* — words entirely composed of consonants, something German voices spoke carelessly into the air, unformed, unstructured. The words "Poles" and "Russians" were placed on the periphery of life, not in need of precision and attention. The Poles had been overrun in a matter of days, there was no resistance to things in the word *"Polen."*

Around the time de Gaulle marched into Paris and took it back from us, in August 1944, Poles had moved into the synagogue and the Jewish School. They had their heads shaven too, and, like the Russians, smelled of disinfectant, the odor of Slavs. We forced them to keep clean, because they were dirty by nature. But in spite of the strong odor that surrounded the Poles, as a matter of fact because of it, I saw the Poles much as I had seen the Russians. Again, I leaned against Herr Heim's carpentry shop and watched the synagogue. My mind chewed the Polish sounds they uttered, guarded by Germans with guns. To enter the synagogue would have corrupted my body, covered it with an invisible film of disease, filled my lungs with the atoms of delousing powder. The Slavs themselves were a disease! I heard someone say the walls of the synagogue had to be constantly whitewashed otherwise they would crumble and breed typhoid. The Poles urinated against them in every corner if nobody watched. Poles were criminals with strange customs, un-German customs, and we children were warned to stay away from them. I hazily imagined being forced to enter the synagogue, cavernous realm of the Poles. I was a captive of its impure spaces, drawn trance-like toward the Polish workers who dominated the building with the Star of David windows: a dreamlike abduction into the forbidden. I wanted to be a victim of the outcasts, thrown among their smells and secret spaces where no eyes of my world could penetrate or aid me. I wanted to be body and mind-abandoned to the desire of the Poles, "the others" that threatened to destroy the known world of the Landwehrplatz if they were given the opportunity. My mind enveloped the disinfected spaces of the synagogue; my skull became the wall of the mutilated structure. Poles, Russians, and Jews grew out of excrements; they carried the rich odor of unchecked and forbidden bodies.

— *winfried weiss* —

⫷36⫸

During the summer of 1944 enemy planes ploughed through the skies of Germany as if they were spring meadows. The allied armadas hung like clusters of heavy grapes and turned the blue skies of Franconia gray with their contrails. Mosquitoes flew ahead and dropped flares, bombers followed and dropped bombs. In June the USAAF dropped more bombs then ever before, even more than the RAF; in July, the American tonnage dipped a little, the RAF's went slightly up, then the bombing fell, with a low point in January 1945. But in February, when spring was in the air, enemy planes came back out in force like swallows. We had so many alerts that we no longer bothered to undress when we went to bed. The time between the sirens and the planes got shorter and shorter. Some people had started making beds in their shelters.

On February 13 and 14, 1945, we sat in our own cellar together with strangers from the street and listened to endless fleets of bombers, Lancasters, roaring overhead on their way to Dresden. People looked up to our whitewashed ceilings as if they could penetrate them with their eyes and shook their heads. They spoke only in whispers; nobody had ever heard so many planes. The Linden Square was filled with rumors of what happened in Dresden.

They said that 150,000 people died and corps were heaped in the street waiting for bulldozers to push them into mass graves. Dresden had been reduced to a smoking rubbish heap and it could happen to us at any time. We stored more buckets of water and sand in our shelter and in the hall under Hitler's portrait. I got more and more obsessed by the thought we could get trapped in the cellar and burn to death. While bombers droned overhead, I felt insignificant, like a rat trapped in the cellar, as Frau Beyer kept saying. We sat underground eternally.

By the middle of February, school hours had been reduced; they needed our teacher for the final victory, they said. We went from eight to ten in the morning and then left school. I had started to write essays for Frau Baumann; on February 23, we wrote about the German farmer and his importance to the people.

February 23, 1945, started out like a good day. It was warm, the air smelled like spring, and buds on the linden tree were beginning to swell. I wore knee pants and white socks, and remember distinctly how warm the sun felt on my naked knees. My knees remember well. There are records to confirm it. The meteorological station in Frankfurt/Main issued a mild forecast for the day: high pressure area extending from France into southern Germany, visibility 10 km. There were southwesterly winds at 10 km per hour, weak and pleasant. Temperature was 11 degrees Celsius, very mild for February, portending an early spring. There was slight condensation, variable altocumulus and altostratus. The German code for the cloud formation was transmitted as 412-5-7-88405 to prevent the Allies from using our data for their bombing.

It became a blue, clear day. The sparrows in Linden Square fluffed themselves into round balls and chirped. Winter had passed. Franconian fogs were gone. In our dining room we still had our Christmas tree from 1944; it looked like a relic, a dry skeleton with ornaments from another time. The room had been too cold, we had no fuel, so nobody had taken it down. My mother kept saying it was a disgrace and she hoped the neighbors wouldn't see it; it wouldn't have happened if father were still here.

On the Landwehrplatz we sat in the sun; Rolfi said that the Luftwaffe had stationed new jets on our airfield. The jets were going to sweep the Americans from the skies; the Americans were cowards anyway; they had no discipline; in our apartment my mother was cooking dumplings, because she had gotten some meat that morning; it was going to be a good lunch for a change. Dresden had disappeared in the blue day. The air seduced our souls to grow wings the only way we knew — as airplanes. Airplanes triumphed over gravity: Rolfi and I were gigantic FW Condors. Their powerful four engines pulled us steadily above the earth's impure condensation into the ether where we leveled off and serenely circled Europe and points east. Anneliese was an enemy

Lancaster and Margarete Riedel an American DC-3 trying to sneak in paratroopers.

Rolfi and I bombed Kiev; our shiny wings swept upward as the bomb load was released; we circled once more: the onion domes of Kiev were burning. We became Me-109s and shot down Anneliese whose greasy pigtails wobbled in the spring air as she tried to escape us. But all enemy planes were shot down; only Germany planes reached home safely. Her engines were on fire, her crew bailed out. Our pursuit was merciless; our mechanics had installed long-range fuel tanks; we couldn't be stopped.

I cut through the sky like a sharp blade: all speed and altitude, drunk with the sunny air. I was the edge that sliced through the icy spaces above Russia; I parted the hot air over Tunisia that we reconquered for the Reich. We skimmed with dizzying speed over Siberia's tundra. Our eyes were cameras that scanned the ground for enemy activity; we saw all. We conquered the world by air. But we forgot to turn our eyes to the spaces above because we thought that we were flying higher than anybody else. At two o'clock high, hundreds of silvery bodies emitting white contrails streamed toward us in the unobstructed skies.

37

The Americans sounded the trumpets of the Last Judgement! Archangels were humming at the gates of Kitzingen, the air parted before them like the Red Sea. The Americans had launched Operation Clarion to destroy all railway centers in Germany, and fate had already given us a day of reprieve. On February 22, 38 B-17s were sent out to attack us but couldn't find Kitzingen. Early the next morning, 452 B-17s took off from southern England. They flew at an altitude of 20,000 feet right into the German Reich. While I was writing my essay for Frau Baumann, they had crossed the Schelde River through light cumulus clouds, but Franconia was perfectly clear. The angels of destruction appeared in metallic flashes of combat wings gliding into central Germany while we pursued Margarete's pigtails. The first Air Division was scheduled to attack the cities of Bayreuth, Eger, and Plauen but had difficulties with their targets. Therefore, they turned southwest where I was an infinitesimal speck in the larger definition of "target of opportunity."

At 11:15 a.m. , while my mother's potato dumplings were expanding into light fluffy balls in softly boiling water, our sirens went off. The Russian steppes, the minarets of Tunis, and the blue waters of the Atlantic vanished like mirages and we ran to our potato cellars. The sparrows we left behind in glorious isolation. Doors slammed, a car screeched, the square grew quiet. The pre-alarm warning left the world waiting for the beating of the wings.

The external world was silent, but the interior of the houses banged with noise and confusion. The Reidels were dragging out their suitcases, Gertrude stood at the window and listened for airplanes, and my mother said that everything was *beschissen*, "shat upon," because her dumplings were going to be ruined. Potato dumplings were symbols of the ordinary world to me, now on the brink of extinction. We sensed disaster. After the 23 of February 1945, I began to believe that sunny spring days were actually traps. Behind the sun unknown terrors were waiting to be unleashed just when I thought myself the safest. We ran to the dining room windows, the Christmas tree dropped needles as soon as the draft hit it. We could hear distant airplanes, guns boomed in the northeast. The sirens wailed a full alert. God descended to 13,500 feet.

The entire gendarmerie ran into the hall at the same time. Gertrude reached the bottom of the staircase with her suitcase, I was separated from my mother by the Riedels. Frau Riedel held onto the railing. She had Rainer on her arm; he had been born six months earlier. She blocked my mother from reaching me. The Riedels had gas masks around their necks; we had forgotten ours. Above us the sound of airplanes sent vibrations through the old monastery: the A-flight of the 96th bomber group of the American Air Force had arrived. My mother seemed to come down the stairs in slow motion; the lead plane dropped the flares to mark Kitzingen for the whole sky to see.

It was exactly 11:34 a.m. when the first whistle dropped from the sky. The pitch of the sound grew deeper as air seemed to rush faster and faster before the falling bombs; then came an unmeasured amount of silence before the end of paradise announced itself. Frau Riedel crossed herself and her lips formed the word "*Gott*" but it remained soundless. *Gott* was obliterated by a shock of explosions, which we survived thanks to Frau Riedel's sign of the cross. The front door opened by itself and closed again. The gendarmerie shook, windows were grinding in their frames, and the staircase swayed; Frau Riedel and little Rainer lost their balance. Field Marshal Göring fell back from our suspension. My mother reached me and took my hand; we ran into the dark passage as chunks of plaster fell from the ceiling. In a moment of silence I heard the sparrows chirping outside as if nothing had happened. I noticed clouds of whitewash swirling in the sunlit garden before we reached the cellar, past the potatoes, vats of sauerkraut, and piles of firewood: the familiar world shaken and rattled into oblivion.

We, my mother-the-widow, my sister and I, the half-orphans, sat in the center of the cellar, the most vulnerable spot. My mother held a burning candle with her right hand on our little table. We stared into the flame as if salvation was burning in it. Every time the candle flickered my mother put her left hand protectively around it. The Riedels prayed with bowed heads in their corner, and some people we didn't know sat on the ground on the north end.

⧁38⧀

The explosions came in waves. Sheets of bombs, *Bombenteppiche*, "carpets of bombs," dropped from the open bomb bays of the B-17s cruising at 13,500 feet aiming for the railway yards, but the bombs came into town. Mahlchen had her apron over her face and sobbed. I could be saved by becoming a sparrow. I joined them in the sun and escaped death; the sparrows were the ordinary world; they knew nothing of obliteration. How could they chirp with death pounding at the door? I longed for the straps of my leather satchel, but it had been left behind upstairs. I was condemned to sit in the middle of our cellar and endure the dark shaking at our doors.

At 11:55 a.m. , Hitler was still hanging on the wall, but Frau Riedel's braids had come loose. The B-17s had left and we stood in front of the gendarmerie. My sister Ilse came running up the alley with dusty hair. She had been at her typewriter when the military hospital across the street disappeared in dust and smoke taking chunks of park with it. *"Ja, ja…so was, so was,"* she said, her hands describing pointless semicircles.

The Linden Square looked the same, but smoke drifted down on us and the sky was no longer blue. Flakes of ash were falling, and a fine dust hung in the air, which smelled musty, like wet mortar and old walls.

We had been saved. The B-17s didn't get us; the doors of the Landwehrplatz opened, and people cautiously came out to look around, sniffing the singed air and the hazy mild sun. My mother took a broom to sweep up Göring's crushed frame when a soft swelling sound of motors rose from the direction of Nürnberg. We listened with open mouths. We had been deceived; the Americans were coming again. Their planes with the white stars were playing cat and mouse with us. The Riedels screamed; Mahlchen threw up her hands and we all ran back into the dark.

At 12:07, the 40th Wing of the Eighth Air Force arrived over Kitzingen. It had been scheduled to bomb Plauen, but their H2X bombsights had difficulties seeing through the clouds over the target; they diverted to cloudless Kitzingen, where we sat with disbelief in our dark cellar. It was against all laws of decency and probability. Once was enough. Fate had played a trick on us; the Riedels took up their prayers again but they switched to short emergency prayers: *"Maria Mutter Gottes, bitt für uns"* "Mary, Mother of God, intercede for us." The Riedels wanted the Virgin's aid only for themselves, though. They had pulled a blanket out of nowhere and thrown it over themselves. Five big heads bending downward, with one little bump, little Rainer, outlined in the light of our eternal candle. The Riedels were practicing magic in their corner. Their blanket obliterated the outside, even us, in the cellar with them. The ceilings could cave in, but it wouldn't touch the Riedels under their divine umbrella.

We on the other hand felt naked and exposed in the middle of the shelter. My mother held onto the candle as the second act began. The candle flickered in drafts created by the explosions; the flame was warm and alive, our hope in the black rush of destruction.

When the second wave of B-17s and their fighter escorts arrived, parts of Kitzingen were already obscured in clouds of dust and fire. The planes released clusters of 500-pound bombs that dropped into the city making the plaster fall from our ceiling. The Americans saw our monastery as an L-shaped structure below them, the Linden Square as an open space with bare trees, barely visible. But they didn't see me, hidden in the chaos of a dark cellar, breathing in fear and trembling; I didn't want to die, to disappear like my twin, the blood sausage, into oblivion. I was a universe with uncharted continents, unexplored virgin fields. I was a sun, a star, a planet with satellites and moons. I was a glorious body in the dark heavens; I glowed, yet I didn't appear in the American bombsights, or on their cameras as they recorded the damage they had done. The explosions came and went; columns of dust rose into the Franconian sky. Bombs fell into the cemetery where white angels lost arms and legs, and they sent old coffins into the spring air. Corpes sailed across the sun, rotting flesh and globs of decomposition stuck to the walls of neighboring houses. The church built by Petrini was hit; they got the Deuster castle and the shelters where Gertrude's schoolmates had sought safety, and, most of all, the B-17s got Frau Baumann and her clock. One of the planes unleashed the braids, which had sat on her head like a crown of thorns. Frau Baumann ended in a direct hit close to the railway station, the worst place to be. Somebody afterward told us that she had been pulverized. The Americans ended Frau Baumann, my first teacher, and took over my education.

Combat wing after combat wing opened their bomb bays and released their bombs. One of the whistling galaxies fell into the Landwehrplatz. The Riedel's prayers were suspended in mid-air on their way to St. Joseph as the howling whirlwind descended. Horror froze me. Fear rose from my groin and felt I was growing immense as if I were about to escape from my body. I was floating outside my skull. The noise was coming directly at us. A deafening explosion ended it all.

It was the loudest sound I had ever heard. It paralyzed our ears; it was beyond comprehension, beyond any scale of perception. I expected the walls to fall, but although the whole structure shook in its foundations, making boxes and crates fly through the air and old carrots leap from the sand, nothing worse happened. Glass fell outside in the hall and Gertrude said calmly that Hitler must have fallen from the wall, as if nothing else mattered.

The big whistle had hit the north end of the Linden Square. The convent, the kindergarten, shoemaker Kerzinger's house, and Riedmann's bakery went up in a cloud of dust. The nuns said afterward that a huge boulder had blocked their escape route from the cellar, but that a touch with the crucifix made it move. Windows shattered in the other houses and our Christmas tree blew across the dining room.

At 12:20 p. m. , big columns of smoke rose over Kitzingen; the second wave of B-17s had vanished in the direction of France, and we stood with fear and whitewash on our faces on the Landwehrplatz. Frau Riedel opened her blouse and gave little Rainer a huge brown teat to suck on. I looked at him with hidden envy. His gums clamped down on his mother; he wasn't aware of the chaos around him, oblivious like the chirping sparrows.

Soldiers from the destroyed hospital hobbled past the square. They were in pajamas and on crutches, covered with layers of dirt. At the far end of the square everything was in rubble. The bakery front had fallen into the street, revealing the insides of the rooms. It looked like Irmtraud's dollhouse with miniature furniture neatly arranged inside. The Polish workers streamed out of the synagogue to start clearing the rubble and to look for survivors. It was 12:45; Rainer was still gulping milk from his mother's teat; Hildegard had brought her mother a chair when, form the direction of Nürnberg, the skies released another wave of shiny B-17s. Countless, turning, propeller blades made Frau Riedel pull back her immense brown teat and stuff it into her dress. While Rainer's lips were still sucking at an imaginary teat, we ran back into the cellar where my mother's candle still burned.

The third act began; sparse dialogue, lots of sound effects. The Riedels prayed under their blanket while I stared into the candle listening to the shining wings with white stars painted on them. Kitzingen was already covered in dust clouds, but the third wave dropped their bombs right into that dust and smoke. The Americans had the power of life or death. They answered our prayers with fire and explosion. The potato sack in front of the cellar window swayed in the agitated air. The partitions rattled, Mahlchen moaned, and I had dust between my teeth. Our eyelashes and our hair were white; my teeth clicked against each other, and I couldn't stop them. B-17s were announcing the end of the world; the Americans came as messengers of God. Messerschmitts and

Focke-Wulfs faded into history. Zarah Leander kissed a man with impure skin in a meadow; I came out of a shaven Russian's armpit, and a carpenter gave me an apple. Our stored suitcases danced on the shelves; Margarete Riedel changed Rainer's diapers while she kept on praying, "Holy Virgin save us from death!" Rainer's baby shit rose in our cellar through the clouds of humid whitewash. Not long after the air raid, I developed a daydream. I had been abducted by men in a balloon; I was floating at 20,000 feet, detached from everything below. The men, looking vaguely like Russians, Poles, and what I thought were Americans, had total control of my fate while I floated through the heavens.

৷39৷

At 12:50 on February 23, 1945, Kitzingen was completely obscured in a cloud of dust that rose several thousand feet into the Franconian sky. The American planes had dropped 2,195 five-hundred-pound bombs and returned to England where they arrived during the afternoon. They hadn't lost a single B-17. Thirty-one of their flying fortresses had been damaged by flak. Half an hour after their departure, the survivors of the Landwehrplatz had lined up before the fountain in the Linden Square to get water. The women wore rubber boots and started to clean the dust from their houses. I stood on the square and watched soldiers carry stretchers. One had a blackened human mass on it. It had long hair and only one leg. The face was crusted with blood and dust. One of its arms dangled over the side and bounced up and down as the soldiers moved. I wanted to take a closer look. The form reminded me of animal carcasses I had seen, or birds that had fallen along the road and decayed. The woman on the stretcher looked like a torn bird carcass used up by life. It had no horror for me, only curiosity. The prepared remains of Herr Kolb and Lieutenant Nüsslein had filled me with apprehension, the same way the pale pinched noses of the corpses in the little showroom of Münnerstadt filled me with a sort of vinegary disgust. I watched my mother with horror as she greedily devoured the coffined appearance of the old men and women. The mangled form on the stretcher was something else. It was surrounded by activity, just one of the forms that passed the square. Its transformation from one state into another fascinated me. I was drawn to the stretcher to see what could happen to someone who had gone into the cellar the way we did but had come out differently. I stepped forward, as though to see myself, but the soldiers moved on quickly, ignorant of my metaphysical curiosity.

Tangled, rubbery forms were drawn out of the rubble everywhere. But the housewives along the square were already scrubbing their homes. It was like a carnival of survivors; we could enjoy the catastrophe; the dead excited the living; we had been spared. But the three attacks had destroyed our faith in the laws of probability. If there were three, there was no guarantee that there wouldn't be another. While people were still trapped in cellars, rumors raced through the city. Gertrude was the first to catch them. The RAF would come during the night and finish us off with incendiary bombs.

We took the ornaments off the dry Christmas tree. One of the ornaments that had survived was my favorite: a *Hexenhaus*, the gingerbread house of the witch in *Hänsel and*

Gretel, shimmering with silver and gold, browns and reds. As I wrapped it and put it into its box it looked vulnerable, out of place. I had doubts there ever would be a Christmas again. The ornament was a vestige of something from a past that had been blocked out by three waves of B-17s. All past Christmases were swept into the dustbin: dry needles and glittering particles, tinsel and small useless wires. Frau Riedel had said all day long that this was the beginning of the end, *"der Anfang vom Ende!"* A new era had begun. Maybe the gingerbread house would burn during the coming night and put an end to the entire past.

📎40📎

I n the early evening of February 23, while we were eating cold dumplings, we had given in to the rumors and pan icked. We fled Kitzingen with two bicycles and a big bundle. I had my school satchel on my back; I carried who we were: birth certificates, party membership books, marriage license, my father's promotions, ration coupons, and our ancestor chart. Our papers were in order. Our identity was going to survive the RAF, whose bat-like wings were coming for us. At the last moment, my mother stuffed two insurance policies into my satchel. They would pay her funeral expenses; one never knew what would happen, and my parents had paid the funeral insurance since the thirties.

While we pushed and pulled the two bicycles across Kitzingen, I listened for the English bombers. As soon as we reached the Würzburger Gate, we would be safe and on the way to Biebelried, nine kilometers away.

Reflections of fire radiated from the dark sky and lighted our way across town. Collapsed houses and big craters blocked our path. As we passed the Capitol Theater I was relieved to see it had survived. I could even make out faintly in the dark they were playing *Der Bunte Traum* in Agfacolor. With Marika Rökk. Zarah had never made a color film and I had never seen one. The dim outlines of posters and pictures were mementos from the past. There was supposed to have been a performance tonight.

Kitzingen was mainly in black and white with bursts of color. Close to the Würtzburger Gate fires burned in ruins, houses had fallen into the street, and mutilated trees stood out against the flames. We traveled across a night plain; in the unsure light were bottomless craters, only our guardian angels could help us now, my mother said. I tried to see them in the flickering February night, but nothing changed in the dark landscape before me. My mother stood with loosened hair in a tangle of fallen high-tension wires and suddenly stretched out her right arm: "I've seen it all in a dream," she said, "I've seen it all …" My hair began to stand on end and my skin contracted under a cold exhalation and I began to suck the leather straps of my satchel. They tasted like they always did, the B-17s hadn't changed their texture. It gave me hope that we would reach Biebelried where fresh eggs, cows, cabbage heads, and dung heaps would restore the familiar world. But around midnight, we got stuck under the arches of the Würzburger Gate; soldiers told us to turn back because we were walking through unexploded bombs.

We didn't reach Biebelried until late morning after spending the night on dirty straw in an old stable near the Vaters

Lichtspiele surrounded by snoring soldiers. Outside the gates a farmer picked us up with his cart. I remember the horses' breath steaming in the sunny morning as I chewed a leathery apple the farmer had given me. Although the RAF never came that night, still we went on because we decided to play it safe.

◈41◈

I n Biebelried, the cocks were crowing continuously. We were safe from bombs, but it was boring. The boys my age knew nothing about airplanes and Zarah Leander. I didn't fit in with them; they had dirty noses, they always sucked up the snot that hung down to their lips. We stayed with farmers called Wirsing, the name of a vegetable in the cabbage family. They had a huge dung heap in the middle of their yard. Steam rose every morning from the fresh manure that had been shoveled out of the barn and the stable. A big pitchfork stuck in the middle of the heap; the fork had a dark-brown discolored handle the color of the stinking liquid that trickled from the dung heap at the bottom into a cement groove. I watched the Wirsings' old farmhand spit into his hands before he picked up the fork to shovel manure. I made a big circle around the farmhand and the pitchfork; pitchfork and old man were one. One day the old man pulled an apple out of his soiled coat and handed it to me. I withdrew with a chill of horror from the apple. I was sure that I would ingest the old man the moment my teeth cut through the skin of the apple. The dirty farmhand would slip into me and take over my body and soul with his old deformed hands. I ignored the outstretched hand and ran back into the house.

While the Allies moved closer to the Reich's border everyday, I was safely tucked away at night in the Wirsings' old feather beds. I had a big painted madonna over my head and a picture of a man in leather pants climbing a ladder to get into his girl's room. Her face was barely visible in the shadows of the room. They were the last things I saw before the light was turned off. I wondered if the man would climb into the room as soon as the lights were out, and get warm. Our room was freezing, the walls had glittering veins. I rolled up in the feather bed in the slowly spreading warmth that smelled softly of mothballs, my drowsy mind created a hazy floating space next to me, which I offered daily to Ivan.

Ivan was a young Russian prisoner-of-war who worked for the Wirsings. He arrived by truck every morning and left again in the evening. Like all Russians, he had his head shaved but he didn't smell of disinfectant. Ivan smelled like the Wirsings' cows and horses. His heavy Russian quilted coat threw off a faint aroma of the dung heap. His body kept the smell warm. His big coat was like my warm bed. I could curl up in it; it promised shelter and cozy oblivion. His coat was more beautiful than the Virgin's coat that enveloped little Jesus. Everything he pulled out of his coat and gave me I accepted. Nuts and apples I ate at home. When Ivan spit in his hands before he picked up the pitchfork to shovel horse dung, I picked up the shovel after him and helped. The fork had been transformed; Ivan had obliterated the presence of the poor old farmhand. Ivan gave everything a new body, a new taste, another fragrance. He was a big warm stable. The wings of his big coat were the doors to it; once I could get inside, he would close the doors and we would remain in the warm, scented half-dark. Ivan's protection made the B-17s vanish into the endless sky. Nothing could conquer Ivan. He transformed the steaming horse and cow shit mixed with straw into desirable landscapes; they radiated auras around him like the halo of saints.

Ivan spoke German with me: *"Gut Tag, Bub, komm!"* He spoke mainly in commands, and his grammar lacked endings on adjectives. He spoke Ivan, a special form of German that came straight out of the texture of cow shit; his syllables had the shape of his body. His short commands made me follow him behind the barn where he chopped wood; we took walks into the meadow; I took his hand and wanted to slip up his sleeve into the inside of his coat. We threw hay to the horses; Ivan unbuttoned his fly and pissed into the concrete grove that ran in front of the horses' stall. I wore my knee socks and felt little hot specks of Ivan's urine splatter my knees. Ivan smiled and pissed warm circles. I was overwhelmed by the enormity of the event.

I was a tiny version of Ivan, or he was a giant version of me. In his genitalia I saw a landscape I had never seen before; it wasn't the vast expanse of ice and snow of the Russian steppes where my father had vanished; here everything was dark, brown, and warm. His foreskin had the color of bread; his pubic hair was a revelation: jungles and swamps surrounded the source of the glittering Russian cascade that gave me vertigo. The images of Jesus and St. Michael on glossy color plates receded before my eyes; Ivan was better than St. Michael. Ivan squeezed between two pages. He obliterated paper and words by his sheer presence; he grew into an image around which I gravitated; Ivan made my father become hazier, dreamier, sliding into distance.

One boring, long, drawn-out Sunday afternoon, when

Grandmother Wirsing gave me the old family Bible to look at the colored pictures, I got furious at sweet little Jesus. He had blond hair and wore a pure white shift; Jesus stood in Paradise surrounded by the wild beasts he had tamed. Jesus was as thin as the paper he was printed on. Jesus had no cock. That settled the matter. Jesus was nothing. A mere picture. Jesus was overshadowed by Ivan, whose animals excreted life in the Wirsings' warm barn. When Fritz, the Wirsings' old horse, lifted his tail, I saw immense reddish-brown folds and muscles that contracted pink inside: the pink opened and brown liquid gushed out together with steaming green balls that fell into the straw below. Jesus couldn't do that. Jesus had no smells, his body produced no gigantic upheavals. But Ivan's body radiated warmth and smells; he made steaming water. His big Russian quilt coat had the power to cure all illnesses, set all mistakes right, make the sun rise, and evaporate night mists. His coat was a furnace of energy.

When I heard the lonely roosters crowing in the chicken yards of Biebelried, I imagined that they were crowing for Ivan because they were separated from him as I was on Sundays, which were given over to Jesus. I was surrounded by paper flowers and memorial pictures of deceased relatives that Frau Wirsing had stuck around the oval of her living room mirror. That was Jesus! Frau Wirsings' dead wanted to join Jesus, but I wanted to be with Ivan.

⧼42⧽

At the same time as I became apprenticed to Ivan the Russian, the American Air Force took over the German skies. An American fighter appeared out of nowhere and strafed Mrs. Wirsing's eighty-five-year-old mother-in-law walking down Main Street in her black widow's weeds. The old woman was in a state of shock in the Wirsings' big kitchen. People fanned her face and gave her schnapps, while Ivan grinned and said, "Boom, boom." It became dangerous to walk in the open countryside. One day, when Gertrude and I rode on her bike over to Westheim, the Americans came at us all of a sudden. We rolled into the ditch as we had been told to do and listened with pounding hearts as the American planes pulled back up and disappeared.

In the east, the Russians rolled over east Prussia, got Silesia, Danzig, and were headed toward Berlin. The radio said our secret weapons were ready to destroy the enemy. We even had a long-range bomber named New York; it could fly to America, bomb it, and return safely to Germany. This plane had four engines and rivaled any bomber the enemy possessed. But my soul was preoccupied with Ivan, who made the sun rise every morning when he came in his truck. I asked my mother if we would take him back to Kitzingen. My mother had once borrowed a Pole from the synagogue to help her haul some wood. Ivan could do the same. She laughed; I knew I couldn't reveal the secret I had found in Ivan. Ivan would remain a dream. My eyes were full of tears when I climbed into the Wirsings' horse-drawn cart that brought us back home. Ivan stood at the gate and waved; we never saw him again. The Americans liberated him a few weeks later.

Before our final return to Kitzingen, we had already returned once to check things out in the gendarmerie. When we walked through the damaged viaduct, we saw a pile of bundled corpses lying in the sun in front of a small house covered with vines. There was nobody around and my mother pulled me over to the silent bundles on the other side. Somebody had wrapped them in brown paper, but the paper was not long enough. The heads and legs protruded. The corpses emitted a faint sweetish smell. My mother pointed to a small bundle. It was a boy my age with black curly hair covered with dust. He wore boots like mine. His right hand was raised stiffly upward in a fist. My mother said with shining eyes, "Look! He's as old as you are. He's making a fist at his murderers!" And she imitated his fist.

The boy was lying next to the bundled form of a woman whom I took to be his mother. The two forms belonged together; one couldn't exist without the other. They had gone to the cellar as we had, but didn't emerge alive. I, as he, had tied on my boots the morning of February 23; but he never untied his. The innocence of his neatly tied boots flooded me with pity. The small trusting and confident motions with which he had dressed himself in the morning had been rendered useless by noon; sad and pathetic. I felt the same. I wanted to bend down and pull back the paper to see his face, but I was afraid he might look like me. When we left the bundles I was relieved. I had just seen proof that we wouldn't be killed, because the boy and his mother had been killed for us.

By the end of February, rumors raced like epidemics through Kitzingen. Frau Riedel produced an new rumor everyday the way a chicken lays her daily egg. The Americans were coming from the southwest and ran over children and women with their tanks. The Russians were coming from the east and raped every German woman in sight. The English were coming from the north and they were going to burn us all up. In whatever direction I looked blackness was descending. Every time the RAF was supposedly flying toward us, we left with an emergency bundle on one of our bicycles. We had a new method to confuse the enemy: every time we ran, we ran to another village-south, west, east, north-and stayed with all the farmers we knew. Dettelbach in the north, Sulzfeld in the south, Holenfeld in the southeast, Albertshofen in the north, Mainbernheim in the east, Westheim in the west. I was out of breath. Everywhere we went it was the same: an unaired, unused, cold and humid room with icy beds. Photographs of dead grandfathers were on the walls next to naphtha-oozing Virgins and Holy Families. Like Hitler and Göring on our wall, Virgins and Jesus' were gazing into empty spaces past the glittering crystals that had formed on the stone walls. Cheap madonnas with bleeding hearts, crowns of thorns, and tears in their heaven-turned eyes. They ruled the cold empty spaces of abandoned bedrooms in Franconia. Religion smelled like mothballs and stale, freezing air. The scent of cabbage came form downstairs, boiled potatoes, and dung heaps. The tortured eyes of the madonna were the first things I saw when I opened my eyes in the early gray morning. She was permanent in our wanderings, the protectress of abandoned bedrooms given to us. We were wandering phantoms who disappeared after the morning coffee in huge kitchens where I felt uneasy, tired and beggarly among strangers watching every bite I took.

By the middle of March I became nauseous when I saw the clammy Virgins and Jesus' on the wall. I blamed them for my being there, for wandering up and down the Main River. And in spite of the farmers' breakfasts, I grew thinner. My eyes took on a hollow look; it had something of the madonna in it, Zarah, Jesus, and the photographs of the dead grandfathers on the farmer's walls, and the dank vapor of our one-night bedrooms. It puzzled me why the Virgin was always looking into the sky where her son Jesus was said to live. But there was nothing in the vast skies except B-17s, Wellingtons, and Lancasters.

🖎44🖎

During the middle of March 1945, the Americans firebombed Tokyo and killed 100,000 people. About the same time, the RAF appeared in our dark sky and sent us to our shelter. We took up the same positions we had on February 23, the Riedels praying under the blanket, Mahlchen moaning behind her apron, while we stared at the candle my mother held on top of the table. The Lancasters had finally arrived, and we hadn't fled to an outlying village. While the candle flickered under the covert currents that swept through our cellar, the English bombers flew over us and bombed Würzburg fifteen miles away. The soft explosions sounded like distant thunder. The old potato sack in front of the emergency window moved before an unseen breeze. We had been saved again. But Würzburg hadn't.

Clumps of people stood on the Neue Brücke and looked into the western night sky where a sun was rising at midnight: a bright orange glow and yellow flashes that sent out rumblings and pounding thunder. Warm spring breezes rose form the direction of Würzburg where St. Kilian's bones were roasted in a giant furnace. A firestorm raced through the city and gutted everything in its path. Currents of hot air rose high into the night and sent ashes to us and as far as Nürnberg. I heard a man tell my mother a few days later that someone in Nürnberg found the charred remains of a bill with his own name on it; it had drifted through the hot air all the way to Nürnberg. It seemed particularly dramatic to me; it crystallized the terror of the end of Würzburg where I had loved to ride the yellow streetcars with the red city crests. The jellied gasoline had burned thousands alive, they said, or the lack of oxygen suffocated them. The fire storm had sucked all the air out of the streets and people just fell over and died. Burning people jumped into the river to douse the flames and drowned. Rumors said the water was choked with bodies. To my mind, the bombs the RAF had dropped were not chemical and mechanical entities, but an insidious monstrous force. The word "phosphor" — which ate its way through living flesh — lurked everywhere as soon as night fell. During the day, we played "Würzburg" in the ruins of the nunnery; we screamed and pretended to jump into the river, but at night the demons were loose. During the day, we divided each other into enemy bombers dropping jellied gasoline and victims on the ground; during the night, we sat quietly in corners and tried to hear the faintest noise of airplane motors beyond the heavy blackout curtain.

Würzburg smoldered for days after the attack, and we changed our tactics. We no longer ran to villages; we tried to find the perfect shelter. The Beyers' shelter was too close to home; it didn't count. We spread through the neighborhood and tried policeman Bums' cellar. He had a wife and three daughters. Their cellar was meticulously clean, with a cross on the wall; and the Bums prayed quietly under the cross. My mother said she couldn't stand it; we tried others. All shelters smelled alike; murky underground, wet cement, old potatoes, old sand in large boxes in case of fire, walls pickled by years of darkness. We passed old furniture behind partitions, abandoned teddy bears, suitcases that no longer traveled. We couldn't find what we were looking for. We tried the underground bunker of the technical emergency service, but we learned that the concrete walls were too thin.

Our search extended farther away form the Landwehrplatz. We became experts in judging shelters. The farther the shelter, the faster we'd have to run. We finally found total security in a deep old wine cellar at the end of the Fischergasse. Gertrude had carefully calculated that, given a warning, if we ran fast, we could make it in time. Whenever the sirens sounded during the day, we ran with our emergency suitcase and I with my satchel and documents to the wine cellar.

One noon we had a full alert right away. We ran nevertheless, faster than usual. Halfway to the cellar my mother was out of breath and said she couldn't go any faster; but we could hear planes and went on. Colored flares dropped from a silvery shape high in the sky. People screamed and pointed to the floating, exploding lights. Panic broke out in the

Fischergasse. People dropped bicycles and suitcases to make it to the wine cellar. Our calculations were wrong; we would be caught in the middle of the street. My lungs were aching as we ran up the hill to the entrance. Before us was an enormous woman, so fat she could hardly walk. Her immense flabby arms were flaying through the air like windmills trying to propel her legs, big shapeless stumps in slippers. Her legs rubbed against each other and the silk of her stockings made a useless swishing sound. In her red face, two big frog eyes bulged out of their sockets, panic-stricken by the B-17s above, and fixed upon the door in front of us but just out of her reach. Her mouth was wide open like the air-intake of an airplane; it made short rasping noises. She reminded me of a fish I had once seen; somebody had pulled it out of the river, its mouth was opening and closing in futile effort at breathing. Nobody noticed the fat woman. People tried to push her out of the way; my mother said, *"Ach, die arme Frau."* "The poor woman!" but we pushed past like everybody else. Leaving the thrashing bulk behind us; we reached the door and descended into the deep dark cellar: a long wooden staircase going straight down, long sausage-like corridors, vaulted ceilings.

I had all the time in the world to study the walls of this old wine cellar. We spent days in its underground tunnels. The dreary light bulbs threw faint light over the uneven planes of the odd walls. I blotted out what was above by concentrating on the walls. I turned the minute elevations on the walls into immense mountains, forests, cities, cathedrals, swamps, and plains. I bombed my wall-cities with waves and waves of bombers that dropped explosives and incendiary bombs. The cities vanished into dust and smoke. During my silent orgies, I saw to it the cities weren't destroyed all at once. I subjected them to psychological warfare. I allowed them to believe they were secure; then I released my phantom armadas and bombed them again. I played God. I created the entire globe on the walls of the old wine cellar. The whole world burned during our underground stays. I loved destroyed cities. The burning, fully or half-destroyed cities were as beautiful as the rivers and mountains that surrounded them. I created dramatic ruins, burned-out streets with intact facades. These empty facades had grace and drama. Ruins were condensations of their former selves, more exciting and real than whole original structures. Life in my ruined cities was more intense than life in intact cities. In my ruinscapes, trains left on time from one gutted station to another. Their passengers pointed to the ruins and said, "Ah, they got it too...it used to look like..." They spoke with pride. They were excited, waiting for the next air raid to defy me who had unleashed chaos.

On March 22, the German Air Command had hidden the latest models of our jets around our airfield. They were parked on runways cut into the pine forests and camouflaged. It was one of the days we didn't dash to the wine cellar after the sirens had gone off. One hundred and sixty-eight B-17s of the 8th Air Force arrived over Kitzingen and bombed the airfield. The Riedels prayed in their corner again. Mahlchen whimpered under her apron; we sat in the middle of our cellar and stared into our eternal candle. We were our own best imitators. We rattled off our charms to protect us. The next day the Allies captured the Saar region and we decided to move our mattresses into our cellar. Outside on our walls were painted slogans like "Our wall may break, but our hearts never!" and "Death to all traitors!" Hitler and Göring were still stacked against the wall; my mother always wanted to put them back on the wall, but she never did. In our garage my father's green motorcycle was gathering dust next to the black DKW. All the gendarmes had been drafted into the army; they no longer looked after the law in Franconia.

⧉45⧉

By the end of March 1945, I sat on an old mattress in our dark cellar and ate bread that tasted like sawdust. When I raised my right hand, it was not to give my blessing but to fondle my cold earlobes; they made my mind fall into a soft stupor; I forgot my surroundings. Somebody had the bright idea of taking my picture with the last film in our Agfa, just before the Americans arrived. During a quiet moment, I sat in one of our garden chairs in the sun. My mother is sitting on my right on the arm of the chair. She looks twenty years older than she was, with a tired smile. I'm looking into the camera with a doubtful smile. I look rickety, and have two big scabs on my right knee.

We lived off old potatoes, fried and refried in the little lard we could get from farmers, and sprinkled with a few caraway seeds on top. When we were able to get fish we would make soup out of bones, or by boiling onions. Sometimes my mother soaked old rolls and cabbage in water and added spices, which made it taste like meat if we chewed fast. Outside on the square, the linden trees were getting ready to burst into leaves on the first real warm day as if nothing had changed. In the east, the Russians had reached the Oder River, and in the west, the Americans crossed the Rhine at

Remagen. By Good Friday 1945, we lived permanently in the dark illuminated by a thin candle. On Maundy Thursday, we tried once more to get to the wine cellars, but were strafed by planes on the way back. We rushed with other people from door to door, looking upwards to spot the Americans that hopped like airborne rabbits all over the Easter skies.

Easter 1945 fell on April 1. The night before, it was rumored the Americans were only hours away! Frau Riedel whispered into my mother's ears that we should have some white sheets ready in order to surrender. Gertrude said we would all be shot as traitors; we had secret weapons that would turn the enemy away. But nobody bothered listening to her. My mother took out two clean sheets. Frau Riedel said old bed sheets would do; the Americans wouldn't know the difference. A white sheet was a white sheet!

While they discussed white sheets for surrendering, the German Army moved out, and the Air Force School followed. While the gray army trucks rolled down the Landwehrplatz, American planes roared out of the sky and shot at them. Some of them missed their targets and shot into our bedroom windows; a bullet went through a Bavarian landscape into the wall. Nothing was safe anymore, my mother said. Little boys and old men being were being drafted to build barricades to hold off the Americans! My sister Ilse was ordered to sit in foxholes outside the city and watch for enemy paratroopers.

While I sat in the cellar and ate an Easter egg we had colored with onion skin by candlelight, I listened to people talk about Americans who threw hand grenades into cellars where children and women were hiding. Kitzingen was going to be defended! The Americans were going to pulverize us! When we woke up on April 2, we were alone in the old gendarmerie; the Ritters, the Kluges and the Riedels had fled to the countryside. The widow and her half-orphans had been abandoned to the Americans who were coming to loot the city.

🔊46🔊

We had been betrayed! Nobody stood between us and the advancing Americans. The halls and stair ways of the old monastery echoed with guns from the south. Artillery fire rumbled in the distance like lazy summer thunder. Buds on the old pear tree grew heavy as I sat in the cellar and stroked my earlobes. In the north, the German Army blew up the railway bridge we used for our trips to Münnerstadt, then the big bridge in the south was dynamited. A freight train crashed into the river, and the locomotive stood on its head. A wall of thunder and lightning approached us from all sides.

On April 3, Mahlchen from across the street shouted: "Jesus Christ! They are going to blow up the Neue Brücke!" The bridge was at the end of our monastery, and we ran to save ourselves. We didn't want to be alone when the gendarmerie collapsed. We ran into an SS-patrol that forced us into the Bums' cellar.

It was there under the black cross that the earth shook as the Neue Brücke, only seven years old, and the Alte Brücke, 500 years old, were blown into the air.

◥47◤

The world collapsed and St. Gabriel flew through the air to announce the end. That's what Frau Bum had said when the bridges on both ends of the Landwehrplaz blew up in orange fireballs. St. Gabriel sat in a small American plane circling Kitzingen on April 4. He watched the ground closely and then gave the signal: the Americans started to shell us. Long hoarse whistles, then detonations. Houses across the river went up in flames, farmers' hothouses flew apart like spun sugar candy. The Germans blew up munitions dumps and set fire to the jets on the airfield; the barracks in the west burned, and the hospital next door caught fire. The SS was still in town waiting for the Americans. We sat on our mattresses. At 1 a.m. on April 5, my mother said that we had to act now; our secret weapons weren't going to turn the Americans away anymore.

Over our garden the sky bloomed orange and yellow; broad sheets of lightning rose and fell, like the picture of the aurora borealis in Gertrude's *World Atlas*. The guns of the American artillery were shaking the night; sometimes a shell would whistle over us like a glowing comet. We marched into our garden, my mother first with a shovel, then Ilse with two big cooking pots; Gertrude carried a box, and I brought up the rear with our pressure cooker. We were going to bury the Third Reich. We dug a hole under the pear tree as the night burned in a slow fire. We wrapped a blanket around the box with our silver. The looting Poles and Russians weren't going to get that. Then we buried two pots so that we would have something to cook in after the looters were gone. Ilse dug a second hole for our pressure cooker. It had been used for steaming potatoes since my parents' marriage. Now it held our insurance papers, savings account passbooks, ancestors' chart, and my father's documents. In the center of the cooker lay my mother's jewellry including an eighteenth-century silver cupid holding a garland of flowers on an oval brooch. My father's medals were with the angel. The pressure cooker was Gertrude's idea; she said we had a perfect container for valuables and a pot to cook with. The pressure cooker went into the moist ground while an American shell streaked across the garden; we ducked, although we knew it wouldn't hit us. Most of the shells fell into Etwashausen across the river.

From the pear tree we went toward the ducks. The ground was slippery and wet because the ducks always splashed water form the pen. We dug another hole, one we wouldn't open up again. The ducks awoke and flapped their wings. My mother threw in her party membership book, then Ilse's, then my father's. Party buttons followed, black swastikas on the brown ground. A large knife with the SS-emblem, all of my father's decorations with swastikas on them, even some of his epaulettes and then a small caliber gun we always kept in my father's desk. Then we covered the Third Reich. We stomped on the ground, while the night sent out fiery signals, thunder and lightning, and the Americans hurled shells whistling through dark spaces over us. Then we ran upstairs and tied a white sheet to the flagpole.

O ur world was hiding in cellars. Our white sheet flapped for the mysterious Americans on the same flagpole where our swastika had hung. Franconia was exploding: the Germans blew up munitions dumps and airplanes; the barracks were burning; American shells were still screaming overhead and setting the town on fire. I fondled my cool earlobes as though they contained the antidote to the chaos around me.

Götterdammerung. By the time the sun rose on April 5, the SS were shooting it out with the Americans in our garden. We clung to our mattresses in the dark. Machine gun fire, single rifle shots, short blasts of submachine guns. The garden side of our monastery was pockmarked with holes; my tree house looked like Swiss cheese. We suddenly remembered that Hitler and Göring were still big as life in the hall. My mother ran and got them; we shoved them under the sand in the next partition and stuck a few surviving tired carrots over them. Instead of staring into infinity, Hitler and Göring now stared right into the wilted tips of last year's carrots.

The SS slammed the Beyers' big gate and ran off through our hall. We listened to their heavy footsteps and held our breath. They would see our white sheet. But they didn't return. Their footsteps were the last sounds of the Third Reich.

Silence followed. We slowly walked from the cellar, smelled and listened. Were we still German or already Amereican? The sun flooded through bluish-white vapors that drifted through the garden. It smelled metallic and sharp, like gunpowder. Sparrows were twittering in the sun. Like them we had survived again. I prepared for the Americans who had announced themselves as God in the skies. I even heard our garden exhale in a long deep breath after the long strenuous night.

🙚49🙚

On April 4, 1945, at eight in the morning, I saw my first American. Against my mother's orders, I ran to the end of the gendarmerie, while the others still huddled in the cellars of Linden Square. The smell of fire and gun smoke drifted through the air, the sun lit the white cobblestone, and the buds of Linden Square were about to break open. The Americans had come down from their heavenly contrails; silence announced their arrival.

A young American soldier was trying to climb over the Beyers' gate. His uniform was torn, his pants shredded, his thighs exposed. He flung himself against the gate and pulled himself upwards. Nothing could hold him back; he was agile and tenacious. His torn uniform shocked me, it made him suspect and criminal. He had slung his rifle over a shoulder so as to be out of the way for the act of conquering us through the back door. I took in the ruthless shape of the young American trying to squeeze into our garden. I crouched on the ground behind the corner, with my eyes on the soldier who was on the same spot where I had watched the little Russian after the summer storm so long ago. But I wasn't thinking of the past; I already longed for the American future. The American replaced the Poles and Russians.

Our capture came fast: one moment we were citizens of Hitler's Reich, and in the next we belonged to a new world. The Americans swept in silently through the garden, surrounded us and pushed us outside. With our hands against Frau Kolb's red walls, the soldiers searched us for weapons. The soldier who had climbed the Beyers gate frisked me. My heart was beating hard under clothes that exhaled the dank air of the cellar. He didn't notice. He runs his hands up and down my sides and inside my legs with fast expertise and went on to Gertude. Meanwhile, the Americans stormed the office and smashed the portrait of Hitler over my father's desk, which we had forgotten. They broke open the gun cupboard and smashed the guns over the banisters. The guns broke, but the monks' banisters held; then the Americans swept through the apartments. We still stood with our hands in the air, like criminals, my mother murmured, and heard the sounds emerging from the open windows. The Americans aired my father's uniforms, took his saber and black pith helmet form the Weimar Republic as souvenirs, and then crashed through the locked garage. While we had our hands up in the air, they drove off with Lieutenant Nüsslein's black DKW in a cloud of exhaust fumes. When they pulled out my father's green motorcycle, my mother screamed, her hands up, that they couldn't do this, it belonged to my father. They couldn't start the bike. My mother said my father had loved his bike! She had dusted it every week since he left. A black American appeared. We had never seen one. He got on the bike, started it, and drove down the alley. The sound of a sputtering motor was the last sound of my father's past power as it disappeared in blue smoke. My mother cried; who could have thought that a blackamoor would steal the bike of an honest Franconian policeman.

⧼50⧽

The American era began with a tight curfew. During legal hours when people could be outside, liberated Russian and Polish workers roamed the streets looting stores and wine cellars; they threw furniture and bundles out of windows; Germans carried them off. Spring winds blew wrappers through the streets of Kitzingen. We found half a chocolate bar wrapped in silvery foil on Linden Square. Rolfi and I debated whether we should eat it; we were so hungry that our bodies won out and we did. Farmers came with huge vats on their carts and siphoned wine from abandoned wine cellars; liberated foreign workers snake-danced through the streets and shook wine bottles in the Germans' faces. We locked ourselves into the gendarmerie where Frau Riedel, who had come back, said that the bodies of three German soldiers who had been blown up on the Neue Brücke by our own troops were still lying unburied in the bushes next to the hospital. The three bodies drew me out of the gendarmerie like a magnet. I wanted to see death.

While the singing workers went by, I slipped out of our monastery. I followed the Russians and Poles up the hill and around the corner: there they were: three decomposing bodies. I felt compelled to see them as if they would give me an answer. Someone had put them in boxes; they were covered by the spittle of foreign workers. While American trucks and Jeeps passed by, I studied the silent forms. They stank. Russians came by, held their noses, and kicked the coffins. The corpses in dirty gray uniforms didn't move. Their faces were bloated and bluish. Their bodies seemed to be close to bursting in the spring sun, growing like the expanding buds on linden trees.

One of the soldier's eyes were open. He stared like Hitler into unknown space. These dissolving forms were in possession of a secret I had come close to. Behind the soldier's dead eyes were secret meadows. He had thrown his lifeless body like a tantalizing affront before my fumbling eyes. Suddenly I felt I had outstayed decency before the corpses and dashed back to the gendarmerie.

⧰51⧰

On April 9, 1945, five days after the fall of Kitzingen, the last B-17 rolled off the assembly line in Seattle. A crucial period of my metaphysical education came to an end. My eyes no longer searched the skies for angels in oxygen masks that made my teeth chatter; now I watched the Americans in full daylight stringing out telephone cables along Linden Square. Like the soldier who had climbed the Beyers' gate a few days earlier, the Americans on the square assaulted the space before them: they spun wire off their large wooden spools with dizzying speed. Out of nothing they created a system of cables, machines, and motors which hummed and emitted lights, and captured voices from the void. The Americans moved with speed, precision, and powerful bodies: I fell in love with them.

While the German Army still fought not far from us, and while German jets appeared in the sky to strafe the Americans, I became a traitor to the Reich: the Third Reich was on a garbage pile in the hall. We dug out Göring and Hitler from the sand and tore them apart. Pieces of their portraits lay on top of shattered plaster and broken rifles. Someone added the red-inked war chart from the office. The war was over; it was a dusty and unimportant pile of the past.

The Americans had power. They had machines that conquered everything; they were green like their uniforms. Their bodies and machines blended into one. And the Americans had food. Their field kitchen was behind our garden wall in the hospital yard. We smelled American food from our garden. Their kitchen warmed up the air and made it fragrant: abundant food being cooked and a soft edge of burning kerosene with which they fired their stoves. Life was on the American side of the high wall; Germans lined up with pots and pans each afternoon to get leftovers from the Americans who poured the food down the drain before their eyes. Frau Beyer begged for coffee grounds and got them. We brewed coffee with them over and over again until only thinly colored water was produced. We starved, while the Americans dispensed grace according to their mood. I stood with Frau Beyer in front of the Jewish School where German refugees form Silesia lived now and watched Germans beg for food in front of the American kitchen. A black cook suddenly crossed the street and came toward me. I was paralyzed. His gigantic black body was defined by a dazzling white T-shirt. He handed me a large open can of cling peaches: the muscular American body gave nourishment — he smelled softly black and like peach syrup. I was triumphant: he had chosen me! Frau Beyer, who always screamed "God will punish you!" when the Americans poured food down the drain, fell silent in the cook's presence. She stared at us as if a miracle had occurred.

My resistance drained from me and collected like a puddle at the feet of the black cook.

The Americans triumphed everywhere. I had been reborn for them. When I stood with my mother and other Germans on the hastily repaired Neue Brücke in the afternoons to toss scraps of food and our last bottles of wine to German prisoners of war in slowly passing American trucks, I felt like a traitor to the Americans. I watched the American guards, who looked the other way, apprehensively. I wanted what the Americans wanted.

During the afternoons, Rolfi and I strolled along the riverbanks to watch Americans with their German whores. Long lines of trucks and tanks were parked under the poplar trees. The Franconian sun beamed overhead, spring winds came down the river, and trees took on a green halo. Grass along the river was dark green and matted with dandelions. The Americans and German girls were smoking; they laughed and pushed each other down the embankment; the girls inhaled the cigarette smoke greedily and let it come out of their nostrils. A soldier pushed his hand under the skirt and up a girl's thigh. The outline of his hand moved higher and higher. Other soldiers whistled and laughed. The girl raised her leg, a gesture of surrender. She had long blonde hair and wore lipstick. Aryan girls didn't wear lipstick; Rolfi called them dirty whores, and I envied the whores, their Americans. The whores gave us Hershey bars and said: "Come here, little boys, here's something to eat, poor little buggers." They patted our heads and said: "It's a rotten time for little kids to live in!" The girl was lying on her back with her legs wide apart, a soldier on top of her; other soldiers cheered, the girl's mouth was open as if she were sucking in the soldier's presence. "Don't you dare go near the river," my mother told me every day.

"It's an affront to God, what's going on down there!" Frau Riedel said. I went back every day. I wanted to be the whore who captured the American.

The Americans transformed the quiet riverbanks into their territory; their presence was like a high voltage discharge; they left their presence everywhere. They urinated against the poplars; they scattered cigarette butts, cellophane, and chocolate wrappers like seeds into the spring. They sprouted like blossoms on the raw river grass. I gaped at transparent balloons containing a soapy-white substance; Rolfi said the Americans had used them on the whores. The white sheaths contained the disreputable, dark, and beautiful essence of Americans.

At home, Rolfi and I played with the castle, my father's last Christmas gift to me. The castle looked too complete, too whole. Rolfi said it didn't look real because it was completely undamaged. We opened the flap to the back of the main building and stuffed it full with paper. Then we set fire to it. It looked real and alive as the flames leaped out of its gothic windows and consumed the frames; Rolfi imitated the sounds of B-17s that circled the castle and dropped more bombs.

🐚52🐚

When I looked at the Americans I saw miraculous creatures in green uniforms that had the power to satisfy galaxies of unborn desires. Their soul was perfumed with the scent of gasoline and fragrance of warm coffee. It was a matter of reaching behind their wall, of drawing them toward me, but I was insignificant, an overlooked skinny boy with oversized desires. I starved. We survived by selling one of our beds to the farmers, then another, finally our madonna in return for potatoes, some vegetables, and a ham. But there was unlimited abundance on the other side of the hospital wall.

At the same time a twin-engine Arado jet made passes over the Americans. Anneliese Spartz and I climbed into my bullet-riddled wardrobe in the pear tree to observe the Americans. They were shooting at the German jet with red tracer bullets. We had watched them rising from behind the hospital wall like tongues of fire. Anneliese had a faint dark moustache on her upper lip.

My sisters came into the garden wearing bathing suits. They stretched out in the garden chairs under the pear tree to soak up the warm April sun and get rid of their cellar paleness. Anneliese and I climbed down from our tree and visited the ducks, who stabbed their beaks into the water and nibbled at wilted cabbage leaves. I heard a whistle, then another. The whistles had two tones, a higher one and the second one descending in register. An American soldier was sitting on top of the wall waving at my sisters who wouldn't bat an eye. Two other soldiers, drinking out of a green wine bottle, joined him. They hooted and shouted. My sisters remained immobile in their chairs. We looked back and forth between my sisters and the soldiers on the wall, transfixed in our spot between two cabbage patches. Why didn't my sisters answer or respond? I was tempted to do it for them. But the soldiers didn't even look in our direction. My sisters in their polka dotted bathing suits, Ilse's red and white, Gertude's white and pink, looked like two giant geraniums against the brownish walls of the old monastery.

The wall was filled by soldiers. They stood on the wall or sat astride on it, dangling their legs into our garden. They waved, shouted, whistled, and every time my sisters wiggled a toe the wall of soldiers howled like an undulating olive-green wave. One soldier had even climbed on top of the hospital roof and sat perched on one of the stone balls that ornamented the corners of the roof. The whistles and shouts produced no reaction from my sisters. They started to throw things into our garden. Packs of chewing gum—green, yellow, and white, fell into the dormant flowerbeds. Dark brown Hershey bars, entire K-rations, cans of peanuts, gull-green cans of peas, beans, peaches, bottles of wine, applesauce and soups.

Anneliese and I became frantic. We pulled out an old wooden box from underneath the rabbit hutches and flew across the vegetable beds to collect the objects that landed with quiet thuds. A pair of Lucky Strikes sailed across, the biggest prize of all. Red and white. The cellophane felt cool and crisp, and crackled when stroked. My mother, later on, exchanged it for butter on the black market — she always said she could have started a little empire with that pack of Lucky Strikes if she had wanted to, but there were already too many crooks around.

Our box was rapidly filling, and still my sisters didn't move. We scurried on like excited scavengers. The American heaven had opened. A multitude of American hands kept throwing things in our direction. I knew they weren't thrown for me, but I picked them up. I became my sister's surrogate, responding because they didn't.

A can of white beans with ham flew across to us like one of our V-1s. While watching its path, I noticed Frau Riedel and Margarete at the window. Frau Riedel pushed Margarete back into the room and I heard her say loudly: "It's a disgrace for the whole neighborhood!" Anneliese and I were beyond mortality. We ran to collect. The sky filled with objects from the wall, first small, then larger. Anneliese's tiny moustache stood straight up with excitement. We ran after the vision of chocolate, the unattainable. We amassed an immense treasure. Our garden had been transformed into the receptacle of the miraculous. Anneliese's pigtails flew, my knee socks fell to my ankles. I, Winfried, of the perfect navel, twin brother of a blood sausage, raised on foaming milk from the Kuhns' stable, had become a frantic scavenger.

The American eyes focused on my geranium-like sisters, ignoring me. We had to find a second container, an old blue enamel bowl from the ducks. Anneliese told me that I could have all the chewing gum. She knew of a girl who had swallowed chewing gum and it had gotten stuck in her stomach. She had to have an operation. Chewing gum was dangerous.

One of the soldiers standing on the wall started to make funny movements back and forth. The others cheered; more objects came flying. I noticed that Mr. and Mrs. Beyer watched from their bedroom window. They had put a pillow on the windowsill, and, comfortably resting their arms, side by side, they observed us the way one looks at a theatrical performance. Anneliese found a long package of broken crackers.

The soldiers on the wall opened bottles of champagne; corks popped in the air. My sisters still didn't move in their chairs. One soldier threw an Army boot into the garden. My mother rushed out in her apron, towel in hand, and ordered my sisters inside. We watched her towel dance up and down as she talked to my sisters, pointing at the door. When my sisters finally went inside, the soldiers on the wall let out a howl that made the pear tree shake, then slowly climbed back into their own territory.

I searched every inch of the garden several times following that miraculous morning to make sure I found everything. We had missed chewing gum — Wrigley's and Juicy Fruit in yellow wrappers. When I peeled off the paper and dirt, I found tiny sticky drops on the flat, waferlike gum. Ants had gotten to it. I brushed them off and began to chew. It tasted fresh, sweet, and sticky. America smelled like Juicy Fruit gum.

⧨53⧩

My occupation with the Americans became an obsession. While the German armies still tried to throw back the Allies in the west and north, I surrendered my soul to the conquerors. Wolfram, Irmtraud's brother who initiated me into the mysteries of the SS not so long ago, died in his black SS-uniform close to Kitzingen. Rumors of his death and of the fighting made no impression on me. I didn't want the Americans to leave, I had survived into a radical new age. I didn't want the Germans to come back. They were gray ghosts. Their uniforms contained bodies different from those of the Americans. German soldiers didn't have the Americans' shiny, fragrant surfaces. When the fighting army left and was followed by the occupational forces that confiscated the Beyers' part of the gendarmerie, I was ecstatic.

I was heartless about the Beyers' misery; Frau Beyer's tears didn't move me when they were obliged to leave on short notice. The Americans were going to live next door! The tranquil garden days when I helped Herr Beyer water the nasturtiums and drown snails in the bucket were only a faint memory, like the blue smoke that lazily drifted from my father's office. My mother wept as the Beyers were moved into the top floor of the Jewish school across the road. I wanted it all for the new Americans.

The Americans moved into the Beyers' part of the monastery like a magnificent cloud of thunder and lightning! Bulldozers came through the gate and leveled the garden. The Beyers' nasturtiums and snapdragons were flattened out, along with the vegetable beds. Machines spread gravel over the even surface where fat crab grass had once grown. Then a group of soldiers put up a huge kitchen tent in the garden while another group ran back and forth along our fence and put up barbed wire: from left to right, up and down and crosswise. The fence became a metallic porcupine to prevent fraternization.

We watched from the windows. Frau Kluge said this was the end of an epoch. I didn't care. I didn't know what an epoch was. We were breathless by the speed with which the Americans moved. A generator made electricity which the Americans allowed us to share because the circuits couldn't be separated. We were the only house in Kitzingen with electricity. Electric currents connected us with the other side like invisible blood pumped between sympathetic bodies. The Americans installed a loudspeaker system. I listened with both ears to, "You are my sunshine, my only sunshine, you make me happy..." and "Don't fence me in..." The songs drifted day and night over our part of the garden like music from another world.

Our garden had become masculine — transformed into the image of the Americans. As spring burst into leaf, an army of men unfurled before my eyes. Nature and the Americans were the same. The Americans brought longer, lighter, greener days. When I looked out the window, I saw in the Beyers' lost garden soldiers that smelled like gasoline and freshly brewed coffee. It was the male smell, inseparably connected with machinery. The generator behind the hospital wall blubbered day and night; and on Linden Square, a communications system hummed behind panels of buttons and little lights, surrounded by tanks and trucks. Green metal emblazoned with white stares. When I saw a soldier urinate against the big wheels of his truck, I saw the stream of urine as an umbilical cord that connected him with the machine. It was natural. The machinery was as shining as the body of the American, both full of promise and power. I wanted to make a nest in the armpits of the Americans who smelled like Old Spice and spearmint chewing gum. The oil puddles and the smell of gasoline gave me an exciting edge to our games between the trucks, unnoticed by the guards. The guards' appearance heightened the sensation as we crouched in the machinery's shadows to escape detection, which I secretly craved.

The Americans tore up the soil of Linden Square; chains of the tanks had taken big chunks of the clay out of the ground. The Americans had ruthlessly violated the square and taken possession of it. I embraced their domination with all my heart. I rose for the Americans in the morning and went to bed with them at night. All truth and justice was with them.

When they handed some us children copies of *Life Maga-zine* with photos of German concentration camps and told us to show them to our parents, I believed them true without the slightest hesitation, although the adults all said it was lies and propaganda. Germans would never do anything like that! I defended the Americans and said that they didn't lie! I was the messenger of the Americans and wanted to propagate their truths. When Frau Riedel made fun of me and asked me how I could know the truth, I hurled a single sentence at her! "The Americans said so!"

I observed the Americans' beauty. A few days after they had put up the barbed wire in our garden, my friends and I made holes in it and went back and forth to the Americans who held out chewing gum and chocolate bars for us. They smoked Camels, Lucky Strikes, and Chesterfields. Even the smallest cigarette butt was a treasure on the outside. We collected them and begged for whole cigarettes which brought food on the black market. More interesting was the way the Americans smoked. They took a pack of Camels from a breast pocket and shook out a cigarette. Then they lit it between their lips with the light well-hidden in their cupped hands. They held their cigarettes with the burning point facing toward the inside of their hand. Germans smoked differently, with their cigarettes pointing outward. When the Americans smoked, I flowed over to them. I wanted to be consumed by the fire inside their hands whose wrists were bordered by silver bracelets. The tendon along the back of the thumb always stood out clearly when that lit their cigarettes. The click of the Zippo as well as the metal top snapping shut was the final motion that defined a ritual of male pleasure. My eyes danced around the angelic flame. There was nothing beyond the Americans. When Frau Riedel called the Americans *"diese elenden Satansbraten,"* "those goddamned devils," I immediately decided to go to Hell, because without the Americans, Heaven was an empty plain. When one of the big American cooks in the Beyers' garden stuck me into a huge silvery pot and put a lid on top and pretended that he was going to cook me for dinner, I screamed in mock terror; but I silently was ready to be sacrificed for the Americans who lined up three times a day for food.

During the spring of 1945, while linden blossoms mixed with American diesel fumes, I invented a new game, another version of the balloons at 20,000 feet. I imagined myself in an overgrown garden with hidden paths and grottos. In this garden I played hide and seek with the Americans. I was the lure that tempted the soldiers to seek me out in the lush jungle like growth. My mind played the imaginary game over and over again before I dropped off to sleep in the warmth of my bed, while the dark foliage closed behind me and an American seeker.

🦎55🦎

The Americans turned us into black marketeers. It all came quite naturally. We were hungry and had no money. My mother decided to take in American laundry. In exchange for soap and coffee grounds from the Americans' breakfast and occasional real coffee in cans, my mother washed clothes for the soldiers next door. It was illegal from the American point of view and immoral from our neighbors'. My mother hung sheets on both sides of the garden and strung the green American laundry in between so nobody would see it. But everybody knew and was shocked. The Americans were the enemy who still fought our own troops not too far away from Franconia. Our neighbors looked at us askance and their greetings became more distant; I felt a silent isolation. My mother and I were victims again, standing in cold winds on bleak plains. But my apprehension was overcome by my delight to see American laundry ironed in our kitchen. For me my mother's business deal had a metaphysical nature. It was a pact with the Americans' otherness, with the criminal character they embodied as enemies. Their illegitimate nature attracted me.

It was my job to return the laundry through the barbed wire and bring back soap and coffee. My heart was beating as I slipped through the hole in the fence at the end of the garden. Their laundry was a definite connection. The Americans glittered more than ever before.

One night when three drunken Americans broke into the house through the garden door to look for the girls they had seen in our garden; Herr Riedel, to save his own daughters, directed them upstairs to my sisters. My mother, who had opened our door to listen to the whispered conversation below, was enraged. The night they tried to get in, I watched my mother and sisters in their bathrobes push the heavy wardrobe against the door to keep out the soldiers. I looked at them with surprise. Why should the Americans be barred? I was stunned when Gertrude went to the window to scream for help. The Americans fled before they reached our floor. I felt sorry for our departure. I had listened to their fumbling footsteps in the dark as they tried to find our apartment. I would have invited them in and flung the doors wide open.

Our pact with the Americans made our fall from grace endurable; I stood outside the laundry room and watched my mother wash the American clothes. She said she couldn't believe she was doing this! What times we were living in! And father would come back one day and set everything right the way it was before! I was torn between her suffering and my own happiness. I worshipped the power the Americans displayed with lavish magnificence, stamped on the skin of their machines and their own bodies. Passion is always greater than morality. Shadows thrown by the Americans were more mysterious than shadows thrown by the sun in our garden. My dormant desires drew food from the American Army next door like a plant turning sun into nourishment. I adored the soldiers. All attributes of the male that I admired before culminated in the American. Even his uniform, its color, texture, the way its folds threw shadows, was imbued with my adoration. When the success of my mother's dealings with the American soap and coffee grounds spread through the gendarmerie, all the other women took up washing American laundry. Except for Frau Kluge, who said she would never, never stoop so low and do the enemy's wash. Especially the black Americans who were animals and nothing else. *"Damit Basta!"* she said, she would rather starve to death. But I perceived the others' reconciliation with the Americans as a triumph; bringing harmony between the two gardens.

⧆56⧆

The impeccable American officers in their brown jackets didn't interest me. The officers were respectable, they ruled, but I was interested in the ruled. Ordinary soldiers circumvented the rules. I longed for the triumph of crime. My imaginary games were peopled by common soldier's disrespect. I loved their short fingernails and the oil and grease under them; I loved their bodily secretions, the smell of their armpits. Smells were power; grease and oil from their machines were power. I lived in a universe of dominating males; they were continuous action, creating and recreating like gods.

I courted several soldiers in the Beyers' transformed garden — a time of paradise irretrievably lose, a fable that won't go away; the golden age when honey dropped form the green tent in the morning. There was the cook, a huge soldier who could pick me up with one hand and plunk me into his big pots. There was the "other" whose name I couldn't remember, dark haired and always drunk in the evenings; he threw bottles against the wall. There was Edward, a mechanic, and Charley who never wore a T-shirt; his name tags rattled wherever he went. Last was Ray, whose name sounded like "Reh," deer, in German. In the evening, I closed my prayers with: "Dear God, protect Father, Mother, Ilse, Gertrude, Edard, the Cook, the Other, Charley, me, and Ray!" In this sequence, I had incorporated the Americans fully into my enclosed world. I presented them to God each night, and they were my guardian angels when I closed my eyes.

I put Ray last because he was the most important. His name ended my prayer like an exclamation point! I envisioned Ray protecting the rear of those marching in the prayer.

When I watched Ray, I was holding an invisible lamp over him to see who he was, and from where his power emanated. Ray was the acid that etched his own image into my compliant metal. I would never escape his embrace: Ray was the lord of the motor pool on Linden Square.

Ray chewed gum and his breath smelled spearmint. He had white teeth. He made contented sounds with the gum when he had black hair on the back of his hand; his skin had large pores. He ran his hand through my hair, smiled and gave me chewing gum. His identification tags fell out of his T-shirt, they swayed back and forth, reaffirming his presence.

Ray was the great spearmint-flavored mystery in my life. I visited him in his room in the Beyers' part of the gendarmerie. He lived alone in one of the Beyer's former bedrooms. On his cot he had a set of earphones through which the same music came that was piped through the loudspeakers outside. Ray introduced me to American comic books, *Superman*. He smelled like the cheap paper on which it was printed. I sat on his bed and looked at the pictures while he lay on his back listening to the music.

From the window I could look into our part of the garden; the wardrobe in the pear tree belonged to the past I already had forgotten. Ray had his arms under his head, was chewing gum, and looked at me. I had forgotten who my father was and where he had gone. The present and future belonged entirely to the Americans, to Ray. Sunlight shot through with greens. Ray had chocolate and chewing gum next to the Old Spice on the top shelf of his locker. I was allowed to take what I wanted; Ray took care of me. He had fought the war for me; he battled the Germans for thousands of miles to capture me. My small heart with the vast spaces was filled to the last inch with a *fata morgana*, eternal security in an enclosed garden. I, the child, put adult desires into a small circumference, a garden filled with magic objects that breathed, expanded, and contracted like a verdant magician's domain.

Ray was unpredictable. Some days his generosity and

kindness changed into tough meanness; it gave him pleasure to tell me that there was no chocolate, no chewing gum, and I wasn't allowed to check the top shelf from where the smell of after-shave floated down. The top shelf was mine. Ray deliberately and arbitrarily withheld my rights from me. If I tried to force my way to the top shelf, he slapped me on the rear. I didn't question his changeable nature; Ray was the supreme ruler of the universe; he had the right to do what he wanted. His moodiness challenged me to challenge him.

I pulled myself to the top shelf; there was a Hershey bar although Ray had said there wasn't. He had lied; he was lying on his bed, listening to music and reading a *Dick Tracy* comic book. When he saw me, Ray pulled me down from the locker and slapped me on the rear. Then he went back to his bed. His punishment was brief and disinterested for the moment. It pushed me to challenge him further. I defied Ray again, he slapped me again.

Ray had a novel way of punishing. He slapped me with the back of his hand rather than with the inside. It reminded me of the way Americans often sat on their chairs in the garden: in reverse, facing the back of the chair. Ray's hand came down in the reverse too. It was a foreign gesture, alien and American, uniquely Ray's, casual and unorthodox, outside the familiar, a fast swift motion that exploded on the muscle. Pain smelled like spearmint and Old Spice; Ray expelled his scented breath downward as he held me over his thighs, his hands stained by the motor pool.

Outside across the fence Frau Riedel hung up her laundry in our part of the garden; she, a ritual of the known, moved in a dreamlike, padded dimension, cushioned by the ordinary. I moved in a superior space, in the arms of the glittering, magnificent constellation of Orion, the hunter. I hurled English words I didn't understand at him: *asshole, cocksucker* as soon as Ray let me loose. He ran after me, caught me at the door or in the hallway and carried me back to his room. The corridor was empty, soldiers voices drifted up from the big hall downstairs. Ray's identification tags jingled. I stared at them in ecstasy. "That's a bad word!" he said. "A bad, bad word..." I supplied Ray with a reason for my own punishment. His hand came down hard on the word "bad." Ray let me escape. I made him come after me. A soldier came upstairs. We stopped until he had disappeared. We required solitude.

Ray had stopped laughing. He punished harder after each escape. He had a right to inflict pain; I offered it to him. My soul was his; he had the right to murder my body. I challenged him to do it. Ray complied; he captured; he punished; he recaptured. We both fell into a frenzy. Time was suspended. Ray hit me with his whole hand, on my head, my sides, my chest, my legs, wherever he wished, wherever passion sought its goal.

There was no pain: my body burned like a huge flower that opened its petals; each petal unfolded in a wave a fragrant heat. Each petal was a step further into the center of Ray, the aromatic murderer.

🐍57🐍

It was evening when my mother made her discovery. I was getting ready for bed when she screamed, "Jesus Maria!" and pulled off my clothes. While she ran down-

216

stairs to get Frau Riedel, I looked at myself in the mirror; dark colors, Ray's colors, ran from my buttocks upwards in all directions over my body. Greens, blues, reds, sunsets, sunrises, whole landscapes with verdant gardens covered my body. I felt no pain; I felt a content deep glow emanating from my body. I gave off warmth to the cold world, I thought.

Frau Riedel poked her finger into my buttocks. I could feel her breath on my skin. I didn't say anything. They asked me who had done it; I said it didn't hurt, I didn't know. The two women screamed and slapped their hands together in front of their bosoms; they looked like madonnas with contorted eyes beseeching heaven. When I finally told them that Ray had done it, I didn't mean to betray him. I revealed his name in pride: I belonged to him: I was a child of his creation! I announced the news to the entire world; I had been recreated by Ray.

In spite of the curfew, the two women marched me off to the Jewish School that had been occupied by American officers. The Beyers had once again been obliged to leave and move to the outer end of town. In front of an officer in light pants and brown jacket I had to let my pants down once again. Frau Riedel insisted that such a crime must be punished! I cringed, I couldn't look at the officer. He walked around me and bent down to get a good look. Then he winked at me through his rimless glasses. I said it didn't hurt. I felt that I had betrayed Ray. I tried to cushion my betrayal by denying pain. I would deny them the right to punish Ray. I failed to understand the word "crime" used by Frau Riedel; I saw only beauty. I burned with shame because I had revealed the angels' secret; I had betrayed Christ to the woman. I fell silent and refused to say anything more.

Nothing became of the incident. I was told to stay away

from the Americans, but they were an incurable addiction. I went back to Ray. He gave me a Hershey bar when he was in a good mood, ruffled my hair, and slapped me on the rear when he was in a bad mood. Nothing had changed. The spring of 1945 seemed endless; I was convinced it would never end. I had become Ray's second self; I was his lightning rod; it was my natural function; the world had made me for that purpose.

⧉58⧉

I mourned the slow disappearance of Ray's rainbow from my body. The arch between him and me, the sign of our covenant, the symbol of our rights, faded as the spring 1945 went on. The chestnuts came out, burned themselves out in their white and pink blossoms. The lilacs bloomed and died. Gertrude took a picture of me and my mother, the first picture with our old Agfa in the new era. We are standing in the garden in front of the barbed-wire fence. My mother is swinging an ax to chop wood which she had pulled out of ruins; she looks twenty years older than she is. I am standing at her left gazing into the camera with a mysterious smile. I am thin and ascetic with strange fire in my eyes, black hollow spaces beneath them. Ray's window is wide open, but here is no trace of him. He vanished, leaving the jingle of identification tags behind.

In early May, we dug out our pressure cooker from underneath the pear tree. We put a big dent into it but everything was there as we had buried it in the early morning of April 5.

My mother's black market deals expanded. She took in a homeless White Russian woman who had a baby from a German soldier. She took her to the farmers where the Russian woman read palms and cards with a heavy Slavic accent. The farmers eagerly paid in food. My mother got her percentages from each reading. We did rather well with American soap and coffee grounds. When my sister Ilse caught typhoid later in the summer, American soap saved her life. We traded it for red wine and meat, which we smuggled into the hospital's isolation barracks where Ilse lay.

We had also taken in an elderly German couple and their daughter who had no place to go when the American soldiers moved into the Jewish School; also a young woman from Cologne who had connections with the Americans. She always had Hershey bars and chewing gum.

The Aryan Reich officially collapsed on May 8. First Hitler committed suicide; Berlin fell, then came the final surrender. The neighboring families stood in our garden and discussed the news with hushed voices. They said we were in a fine mess now! The Allies had destroyed the Reich; I listened, I didn't care about the Reich. For me, it had long ceased to exist, the minute I saw the American climb over the Beyers' gate. Movements of the big world outside failed to impress me; I had all I desired in my backyard.

When the Americans said that "we" the Germans were guilty, I believed it at once, because the Americans said so. I had placed myself automatically on the side of the enemy in any discussion about the war. I defended the Americans' side, Ray's side. People gave me a curious look. I, a German, infiltrated my own people with an alien point of view. I defended the American point of view indiscriminately. My heart defended their truths and untruths with the same passion.

Everybody in our garden said we were innocent, there had been no concentration camps. The Americans invented it as an excuse for taking away our territories. The war had been forced upon the Germans to allow Stalin to take over Europe. I tried to bring up the pictures in *Life Magazine* again and again, but they all said that the "Amis" had faked them, and that children had no notion of reality and the real world.

By May a new playground opened along the Landwehrplatz. It was a large sunken garden, a kind of moat left over from the old fortifications, behind the Jewish School. A creation of the war. Nobody knew how it began but one day the moat was slowly being filled with the war's garbage. Broken plaster, useless bricks, torn concrete, destroyed objets that had been stripped of their last usefulness. Every day the moat changed its appearance like a primeval landscape undergoing transformation form within; hills became valleys, valleys hills. The moat was a miniature version of the Alps.

My old Aryan playmates form the square and I went over the latest discharges every day. We invited some of the refugee children along, but we had ultimate rights over the new territories, because we had lived there longer. The population of the Linden Square had doubled since refugees poured into Kitzingen form all the lost parts of the Reich.

Not long after the fall of the Third Reich, we played in the moat. A girl form Silesia, another from east Prussia, Heinz from the square, Manfred, son of an elderly couple, Georg, a widow's son who lived tow blocks away, and I. The girl from Silesia had a white ribbon in her hair. We, the remnants form the destroyed Reich, roamed over the garbage of the Reich.

We pulled objects form the dump and feverishly started to build a tent on top of the grassy hill of the technical emer-

220

gency service. We felt compelled to build a house, a sort of nest, in the middle of the ruins, as if we wanted to triumph over chaos. We spent hours on it, polished it with our imagination into a magnificent structure, and crawled into it. It was hot inside, with earthworms crawling over the rotting, moldy tarpaulin we used as a roof.

It was a warm and blue day. The Americans were across the street from us. Their noises and music floated over us, we felt secure and sheltered in our own creation.

But war wasn't over yet; it was watching us with half-open eyes. Our childish fantasy contained a profound shock; death was coiled in its center like a spring waiting for a trigger. We triggered our own destruction. We had built a home over a discarded grenade, probably of German origin. The blue, innocent day had black undersides; it only appeared as sunny and blue. The delusion was blasted apart and pulled me into it black vortex and then vomited me out again.

Someone made a move or gesture that exploded. The light ripped apart in front of my eyes in a gigantic explosion; the blue, sunny curtain was shredded, our existence was a cardboard illusion blown away. The explosion was so loud I instantly turned deaf; in the ensuing, silent space, the tent was lifted into the air and scattered with lightning speed as if God's mouth had blown on it. There was a rush of dark gray matter around me: matter's composition had been profoundly altered while atoms and other particles were frantically trying to slip back into their former structure and gain equilibrium. My organism had stopped breathing. I was listening to chaos.

I wasn't sure if the sun would ever appear again. The exposed parts of my body were bombarded with pieces of shrapnel, but my state of shock made them feel like pinpricks, like benevolent splashes of water spinning off the churning air. The external sensation seemed small compared to the internal shock to my system. I found myself whirling in a metaphysical joke. It slowly penetrated my mind that I had survived. I dimly perceived that individual parts of my body functioned in their customary way; ordinary life still inhabited me. I became aware of the comfort of my surviving body, as though it were isolated form what had just happened.

I registered the first sight of color again: it was blood oozing from between the legs of the Silesian girl and staining the light material of her dress. She was lying on her back, moaning with closed eyes; her white ribbon looked like a squashed butterfly in her hair crushed against a rock. The other girl was crumpled against her bleeding friend. I stood up in the subsiding turmoil. I saw the girl's blood as a sign of life. Heinz was lying on his back, his limbs relaxed in curious angles. His face was covered with large fragments of the shell that had gone under his skin. He had one large gash on his left cheek. Manfred was a blackened heap turned into itself. One of his legs was missing; his eyes were wide open as if they were still trying to understand the sudden reversal of fate; they were staring straight into the sun with out blinking. Manfred's skull was open, and spongy matter was dripping down his temples. Georg, the widow's son, was sitting on the ground with his head in his hands; he screamed while blood poured down his head. His body looked burned and sooty. I had two selves, one dazed, one sharply conscious. I registered the Americans jumping out of every window of the gendarmeries ground floor. Jeeps and an ambulance came streaming toward me as I stood rooted to the spot afraid to move as if any movement could destroy my survival. An American soldier reached me and took me up in his arms, but I started to struggle and scream. All I wanted to do was find my mother. I wrestled myself out of his arms and ran home, not conscious of the blood that covered my body. My mother met me at the door, white as a ghost; she stared at me as I told her breathlessly with a mixture of horror and pride, that Heinz and Manfred were dead.

▧59▧

I was euphoric; people looked at me like a hero; I was the only one who walked away from the bomb! People stopped talking on the square when I passed and pointed at me. I allowed myself to be flooded with light; it drowned out Heinz and Manfred who had been consumed by the black ball of fire. I sat again in Ray's room and searched for Hershey bars. I thought back to the explosion like distant summer lightning. The explosion went underground. My mother had to force me to visit Georg who was in the hospital, blind and unconscious. His room smelled stale, his nostrils were two black holes in the white bandages. They expelled something vile from his destroyed body. Georg's mother looked like a big black bird sitting at the head of his bed. My head started to spin, and I told my mother that I had to throw up. She excused herself profusely and took me out shaking her head. I hadn't dared to get close to Georg's bed.

Months later when we had to leave the gendarmerie, we moved into the same house where Georg lived. When the movers carried the furniture upstairs, I saw Georg sitting in the hall. His dead eyes in his mutilated face turned aimlessly in their sockets; he fingered a toy in his lap. I stood paralyzed on the spot; I couldn't pass Georg. My head throbbed. I broke out in a sweat; all reason fled, my legs refused to move. Georg was the embodiment of darkness and he blocked my way. If I passed him he would extract a terrible price. He was a monstrous creation, unnatural, a devil with two heads. Georg lived on the first floor off a dark corridor. I was convinced he would drag me into his part of the house where demons lived in eternal darkness, sightless, vicious, and vile. I stood in the cold for about an hour, before I put one of the movers between Georg and myself as a wall of protection, and slipped upstairs. For months afterward, I didn't touch the walls downstairs for fear of touching a spot that had come in contact with Georg. Everytime I came downstairs, I checked first to see if he was there. I spent hours outside avoiding Georg who sat in the hall learning Braille. The very sight of him and my mind was stultified, any impulse to squeeze past him silently in the hall was overwhelmed. A constant, dim awareness lingered in my mind that a monster lived downstairs, waiting to destroy me. My agony ended only when Georg was sent to a school for the blind far away from Kitzingen.

In the early summer of 1945 shortly after the bomb had erupted, I resumed my life in the Americans' garden. Ray took a knife and removed small shell fragments lodged close under my skin; the doctors had said they would work themselves to the surface as they dug out bigger pieces form my forehead and cheeks the afternoon following the explosion. Ray scraped the knife's edge over my shins and metal pieces popped out; the big pieces in Heinz's body would stay their forever. They would drop off of the rotting flesh and rattle in his coffin. Heinz and Manfred had been buried two days after the explosion on a hot and humid day. I didn't want to go, but my mother insisted. She said it was the proper thing to do; I was the only survivor who could walk.

Heinz's coffin was open. He had a drained white face. They had left a big black piece of shrapnel in his right cheek. A fly crawled over his nose; I watched to see if it would go inside his nostril. I instinctively rubbed my nose as if that could chase off the fly, but it kept on crawling over Heinz's lifeless face. Heinz's face had a strained, tight symmetry. His mother stood at the head of the coffin and told me I should thank God on my knees! I smiled. It was my due to be saved from the black vortex; I was the chosen one to live in the light and with the Americans.

Manfred's body had been so mutilated that the coffin was kept closed. His parents were old and would never have another child, my mother said. They stood at the shut coffin. When I came to make my condolences, Manfred's mother began to sob and turned away. Her husband put an arm around her and gave me an angry look. His face was filled with impatience and hostility as my mother mumbled something, and he said thank you as if he wanted to chase us away. But I was ruthless. Manfred had a huge toy collection; everybody on Linden Square envied it. He had planes, trucks — everything he wanted. Not long after Manfred's death, I asked my mother to ask his parents if I could have his toys. My mother looked at me speechlessly and told me this was a terrible thing to ask. I didn't understand. Manfred was in his grave. Rolfi had told me that dead bodies would expand, become bloated and explode with time. He couldn't play with his magnificent toys anymore; they gathered dust, but I was alive! I could use them! I breathed and lived; Manfred no longer stood in the way of gaining possession of his toys, but my mother said his parents would take his toys with them to their graves rather than give them away. My egotism knew no limits; after all, the same bomb had left me alive with only minor scratches.

Manfred's toys floated like miraculous treasures before my eyes. To possess them would exorcise the last traces of the terrible vision of the dark hole. Manfred's toys were the laurels for the survivor who had escaped virtually unharmed whose guardian angel had enfolded him in his deep wings. I thought I had rightfully inherited Manfred's toys. But I failed in my attempt. The shelves of rare toys stood useless in Manfred's vacated room; their painted metallic surfaces remained beyond my reach. I made several running starts to get my hands on them, ignoring all previous reactions by believing any new attempt would simply cancel out past failures. When nobody moved to hand over Manfred's toys, I turned against his parents; it was their fault, they deprived me of the pleasure. I looked the other way every time I say them on the square.

§60§

*Z*arah Leander always traveled in her films. Her liquid, mystic eyes always gazed toward new shores. Her longing soul was in constant motion, desired by men who ultimately ruled her. She was their victim, body and soul.

In the summer of 1945 I traveled the roads of Zarah, a spontaneous voyage into the misty, northern forest of Franconia. I crossed the promised land, traveling with the Americans.

While the Americans still fought with the Japanese on the other side of the world, and while the Americans used their new bomber, the B-29, which had never appeared in our skies, the troops stationed in the Beyers' part of the old monastery went on field exercises in the north of Kitzingen. I heard it from Ray and from rumors around Linden Square. Ray said they were going to Bad Kissingen, a few miles form Münnerstadt, where Aunt Dorothea had all the food in the world. Uncle Adam had been sent to prison the year before for poaching in someone else's forest. Field Marshal Göring's hunting laws, the best in the world, as Uncle Adam always said, had caught up with him. Uncle Adam was back out and claimed he had been sent to prison for political reasons.

Public transportation didn't exist in Germany, so my mother conceived the idea of traveling with the Americans, which was illegal, but all of Germany was living illegally in one way or the other. My mother talked to Ray whose laundry she washed. Ray said it could be arranged. I was in a state of suspense; I ran a fever of anticipation: the Americans and I were going to travel the same way. The voyage would weld us into one.

By the time we left our party had grown. There was my mother, Gertrude, I, a refugee woman and her little daughter, and another refugee woman. We stood under the arch of the Neue Brücke after dark and jumped into two jeeps at the rear of the long convoy. Ray drove one. I sat next to him on my mother's lap. Gertrude and the refugee woman were in the back. The other woman and her daughter followed in the last jeep.

We rushed through the cool summer night along deserted country roads. We were wrapped in blankets and I watched dark trees and bushes fly toward us in the headlights, become defined, and turn back into black forms soon as the lights stopped fingering them. I was tired but I couldn't fall asleep. My mind was blown by the wind that rushed into the open jeep; I watched Ray's face from the side. He was faintly illuminated by lights from the dashboard. I was in an American vehicle, steered by Ray to whom I belonged with every shred of my body. The women screamed "huh" when Ray screeched around curves; Ray laughed, I laughed. He wore a helmet, chewed gum, and smoked Lucky Strikes. He controlled the jeep like his own body. It was his magic that hurled us through the dark night, through unknown territories with a goal somewhere toward morning. Ray carried me off into his empire where time and space would vanish, where only Americans existed. I had forgotten about Bad Kissingen and Aunt Dorothea. I was traveling in olive-green machinery dominated by the white star in the middle of the hood: an abbreviation everything American, a coded signal for security, a star that radiated the male sex. It had the essence of Ray dissolved in it and was therefore angelic: I was little Jesus riding into Egypt in the arms of demigods that conquered the night for me. The humid cool smell of night, sweat, spearmint, and Old Spice. There was nothing behind me, everything before me.

•   •   •

The Americans had lied to us. When we arrived early in the morning light, we were far away from Bad Kissingen and there was no way to get there or back home. My mother's hair had come loose; it was hanging over her shoulders as she looked around with big eyes and asked us: "What have we done?" I didn't care; we had to stay with the Americans in the forest. I saw the American camp through the trees in a clearing; the morning air was full of coffee, gasoline, and fresh dew. We were connected with the Americans and they with us through an illegal act. They had to keep us hidden and we did our best to hide ourselves. We were both in an illegal position. It was a perfect situation: we lived in a thick, dark forest among giant ferns and leaves that looked like rhubarb with the American camp not far away. The Americans took care of me: they built a small fire and brought food three times a day. I slept under green American blankets that kept the night air out.

Days and nights came and went. The wind sighed overhead through the oaks and birches, dry leaves on the ground rustled; we slept close to each other in a circle. My mother kept saying she wouldn't survive this if the neighbors found out what we had done. It was worse than being gypsies in a green wagon. I watched the sun move through the tree tops and movements of the Americans in their camp. I was in the garden of paradise. Ray gave me an orange; it smelled like after-shave. He brought us coffee and marmalade. I was going to love soldiers and mechanics forever. Ray carried over a big canister; we heated water and he gave me a bath in it behind the giant rhubarb leaves; the forest was green with sunny spots, Ray splashed me with water and we laughed.

One day some village children stumbled across us by accident. They stayed in the distance and stared at us like apparitions. We were sitting around our fire while one of the drivers played his guitar for us. I looked at the children with pity and contempt: they were excluded from paradise. I stood in the centre of the universe protected by a green curtain shot through with sun. The forest mirrored beautiful lost ages. There were no dragons; all monsters were asleep deep in the

229

earth. In God's enclosed garden, I was blessed; the poor village children stood outside the walls and suffered. We were
the righteous who had triumphed by having left the sphere
of the proper and legal. Those few days in the woods seduced me — the forest surpassed all beauty. It was terrestrial
paradise. Eternity would be perfect in this form.

Our stay in the forest was the apotheosis of that miraculous summer when the Americans descended from heaven.
Afterward we went back to Kitzingen in the kitchen van.
Ladles and pots banged against the walls each time the truck
hit a hole. As we came closer to Kitzingen, my thought went
backwards to the woods where the ashes of our fire were still
warm. I never discovered exactly where we had been; it was
somewhere at God's door.

One morning it was all over. On a late summer day in
1945 (the leaves of the Landwehrplatz had already lost their
early green), I came downstairs as usual and found the square
and the Alte Finanzamt empty. I had come down for Ray and
found a gaping space. The doors and the windows of the
Beyers' part of the old monastery stood wide open: the Americans had left. Winds blew chewing gum wrappers along the
street.

I stood alone under the old linden trees and watched the
last trucks leave. They gunned their motors as they went up
the hill to get onto the Federal Highway 8, to disappear forever from my life. Edward, the Cook, the Other, Charley,
and Ray left me behind without the slightest warning. They
abandoned me, disappeared into the night and fog. The only
proof that they ever existed was in my loving memory.

Oil puddles and grease spots stained the square, last remnants of Ray and our short past. Something irrevocable had
been lost. The heavenly American motor pool on Linden

Square had closed its gates. A paradise where white stars glowed like huge turfing daisies vanished while I slept. I had been orphaned for a second time.

My fathers, brothers, lovers, apple gendarmes, Ivans, and carpenter-apprentices had packed up and left. The dimensions of the square grew smaller and smaller. The houses of the Landwehrplatz with their oversized roofs refused to change into something else; they were what they were. Foreign conquerors had conquered me and left me masterless. They left a myth behind, theirs; my mind was aching with it. The rubble around me reflected my despair and resignation. Nobody could soften my sorrow. I had to keep my pain a secret to the end of time. There would be no healer. The ones who could save me had put miles between themselves and me; every minute was increasing the distance, until it was no longer conceivable for me to imagine the space they were covering.

I had been seduced by machines, gasoline, chewing gum, and after-shave; the cool mastery of technology, cigarettes pointing to the inside of their hands, tattoos and green undershirts. My lungs were still full of the fragrance they had taken with them; their scent was vanishing into the morning air.

The melancholic images of Ray and the others, their transfigured selves, still lingered in the empty rooms of the federal tax building. The walls still exhaled the recent past; they mocked my sorrow. I stood at the door and saw empty wrappers — Wrigley-green, Hershey-brown — on the floor, and a piece of black cable, useless, purposeless in a corner, a shadowy reflection of what once had been, a broken remnant itself.

I felt homesick for a home that didn't exist. I was an insignificant form whose soul was torn by the wheels of machinery beyond anybody's control.

231

Sparrows were hopping in the dirty clay of the square, the leaves already a little worn; Frau Lachmann's bedding hung outside the window to air. The old federal tax building, its doors, its windows, were the wide-open eyes of the empty Garden of Eden.